To Emily
Thankyou fer
making happy
vaK!
MickX
Jan 2020 .

Making
Happy
Work

CONTENTS

ABOUT THE AUTHOR

Mick Timpson is a senior meditation and yoga teacher. He is a writer, university lecturer, award-winning artist and architect. Mick is the founder and CEO of **beanddo**, a company focused on delivering modern meditation training to help people, communities, organisations and businesses thrive. He has designed the **beanddo** programmes and leads many of the courses.

Mick has taught design and led teaching studios in many schools of architecture. He has also managed a number of commercial architecture studios including his own practice. He is an experienced speaker on the subjects of architecture, creativity and wellbeing. Mick has also taught yoga, meditation and wellbeing to countless students. The origin of **beanddo** can be traced back to when Mick realised that he had been talking about the same thing to each audience – how creativity, flow and happiness are linked to making happy work!

Dedicated to Sue, who steers our happy ocean liner.

Fig.1 Follow us on social media using our hashtag and help make happy work

"My fate cannot be mastered; it can only be collaborated with and thereby, to some extent, directed. Nor am I the captain of my soul; I am only its noisiest passenger".

Aldous Huxley

INTRODUCTION

Designing Inner Change

As an architect, the first part of my career involved empowering others to design and shape their external world for positive benefit. Now with my modern meditation training company, **beanddo**, I am empowering people to design and shape their internal world for the better — to make inner changes by empowering their own inner architect.

This book is based on how we do it.

Just as architecture is a 5000-year-old art and science for designing the outer world, there is also another 5000-year-old art and science for designing our inner world. **It's called meditation and it comes from tried and tested, timeless teachings of wellbeing, insight and creativity.** When practiced thoroughly and consistently, it is possible to make real change from the inside out.

Everything in this book is based on the **beanddo** 'make happy work' modern meditation programmes, which are designed to help everyone embed and expand the benefits of meditation practice into everyday life. Our programmes are designed to **make happy work**; to help develop modern meditation practice for the busy, active person (which is just about all of us).

Like all good design, the making of an effective and meaningful life is a matter of discovery, not invention. We work with what we have, what we do, where we are and what we know. To make progress it's simply a matter of shifting our perspective towards what is already there, but in many cases it is hidden away and out of view. You and I already have all the resources and materials needed to change, know and be our best selves.

So by empowering our inner architect we can start to make our own world work beautifully, right here, right now! Making inner changes is a process; but knowing we already have what we need is the best place to start from.

How to use this book

In this book, we take a step-by-step insight into the art, science and application of modern meditation. Part 1 looks at the art and science, and part 2 in to how to apply it. Don't feel that you have to be constrained by the structure to make progress. As we say in our meditation classes you can just dive in. So if you want to look at the practical aspects first then start with part 2. The purpose of this unique **beanddo** meditation approach is to shape, direct and combine this powerful ancient science of Being into the modern world of Doing. There are no special mantras to memorise, no raisins to chew, no particular breathing techniques to practice or challenging postures to master. The **beanddo** process can be utilised anytime, anywhere. That's the whole point.

There are written meditations in this book to aid your practice; if you would like to also hear them as audio, listen to my guided meditations online:

www.beanddo.co.uk/guided-meditations

This book is based on the modern meditation courses I run in schools, businesses, and communities. It is designed to support and provide you with the tools to help yourself and others live a happier life. The practices described here are not substitutes for medical care, and if you are receiving treatment you should consult your medical professional.

It's a journey.

If we are going to successfully navigate the meditation path, and what it can do for us, we will need a map:

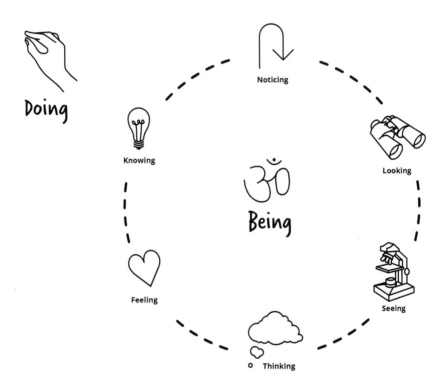

Fig 2. Mapping our conscious adventure from the outside to inside and back again.

From the outset you might notice the map doesn't look like a map. It doesn't show routes, or lead to a particular destination. That is because you are both the explorer and terrain. The journey is a conscious adventure inwards and outwards. Study the map for a moment. You can see there are three parts woven together: an inside, an outside and then something that separates these two from each other. You can see there is an inner centre which I have called, 'Being' and an outer location I have called, 'Doing'. They might appear to be separate but in fact they rely on each other for their existence.

You'll notice the separation is created by a ring of six other locations – Noticing, Looking, Seeing, Thinking, Feeling and Knowing. They are to do with how you experience and shape the journey. This outer ring of perception is basically 'you', or more accurately, an outer enclosing wrapper of physical and mental stuff which filters your perception and how you respond to the world. In other words your mind, body and senses. As you go through this book try to keep in mind this distinction between mind, body and your inner and outer experiences.

The first part of this book introduces some of the core background and tools you will need to start your inward meditation journey.

The second part of the book looks more closely at each of the mapped locations and how through practice, you can develop deeper conscious strategies, which will naturally lift self-created limitations that prevent you from feeling balanced and whole. With practice you can develop insightful and knowing tools which break down and change that outer wrapper so that you join your inner Being with your outer Doing.

As you venture around the map you will begin to find and recognise some familiar and some not so familiar markers and way points.

Noticing – We begin to learn how to stop and explore our mind-body connection, being present in the moment, feeling the shape, space and sensation of the body.

Looking - We turn to look at the body breathing in a way that encourages us to direct and hold attention with purpose, but without interference.

Seeing - We begin to observe and be with passing experience of wherever we are, whatever is happening, to help build a deeper awareness of us and the world moment-to-moment.

Thinking - We begin to change our relationship to our thoughts, creating a positive detachment, in order to achieve a deeper experience.

Feeling - We become liberated from being held hostage to our emotional states and how they make us feel, and begin to understand more about ourselves.

Knowing - A deeper insight into our real potential as we begin to reconnect to what is at our core.

Being - A place of inner stillness. A point of pure being beyond thought, action and external conditions.

Doing - We learn how to utilise our meditation discoveries in our daily actions in the world. Whatever we do becomes a meditation, enabling us to flow and thrive.

Well-known Indian yogi Sadhguru, in his book 'Inner Engineering. A Yogi's Guide to Joy', tells us this is a journey where we eventually see life differently, beyond our limitations and come to know inner joy and peace every moment. It might seem to you that superhuman qualities in every moment are required to meditate and go on this journey. Not true, he says. It is simply just rediscovering that being human is super.

So try it. Sit down. Follow the map and instructions in this book. It will be your first step in taking back control and collaborating with your destiny as you move from an unconscious reaction to life to a conscious response to being alive!

We begin to let go and **notice** where we really are. Then our capacity to **look** with intention and **see** with clarity begins to grow. From there, perception changes and awareness builds so that we see **thinking** and patterns of thought, and how in turn they make us **feel** and react to the world. Once this cycle is observed, insight grows and we begin to **know** a deeper experience that rests underneath our thoughts. This brings us to experience an inner peace, an innate sense of **being**. The still-point within, full of abundance, joy and creative potential. And then with practice, we release it through our **doing**.

Let's make happy work!

beanddo [be-and-do] verb

being and doing. A purposeful merging of the science of effortless being with the art of spontaneous doing, as a way to promote deeper awareness, wholeness, wellbeing, joy, intuition and creativity.

PART ONE

1. Being Different and Doing Differently

All meditation practice is designed to do one thing. To help us experience life moment-by-moment; there is a space of stillness that exists in the centre of our life — **our sense of being**. That's the inner part of us that knows who we are and where we are going. It's the source of our creativity, happiness, wellbeing and insight. For many however, this goes mostly unnoticed because we are distracted most of the time by external things. We are **doing**, mostly at the expense of **being**. This distraction leaves many of us in a state of imbalance.

All we need to do is to build awareness and open up the real meaning of what we are experiencing every day. With practice, the **beanddo** techniques are designed to help us develop that deeper sense of awareness, joined to the everyday activity of life through a **sustained connection to the present moment**. This leads to nurturing a sense of stillness (Being) at the heart of day-to-day activity (Doing). Learning to weave Being and Doing together through the make happy work modern meditation programme leads to reduced stress and anxiety while self-awareness, creativity and empowerment grows as life takes on a deeper, effortless and more meaningful dimension.

Regular meditation practice boosts energy, improves sleep, builds mental resilience and clarity. It eases negative thoughts and emotions and nurtures positive ones. Meditation will even enhance your work, helping to improve focus, creativity and insight.

This is because meditation practice will help you see and act in the world differently. You access higher states of **Being**, which is then expressed through your **Doing** — a deeper consciousness and awareness that is the source of your natural insight, sense of purpose and creativity. You awake to a new sense of optimism and momentum in your life. You will radiate creativity, joy, connectivity and compassion.

When you learn through meditation to be whole – to link that sense of Being with your Doing – you begin to flow. You experience an all-embracing sense of oneness, helping you to feel intimately connected to that inner part of yourself, to that part of you that is never hurt, angry or lost. And in the same way you will connect to others too, in what you do and in the world around you.

Everyone will benefit from your efforts.

However, to achieve this it means turning up. Being present. Being right here, right now. That is both our starting point and our destination. We will travel and explore new dimensions and perspectives, change where we are and how we are, without even moving.

This is why meditation exists. It's deeply rooted in the knowledge that we all want to change, to be better. You may wish to either overcome something that you know limits and compresses your life, or instead grow into your natural potential and move towards finding more momentum and meaning in your life. You will find that both of these motivations are in fact the same. Reduce the obstacles to growth and change will happen naturally.

2. A short note on Mindfulness and Meditation

Is there a difference between mindfulness and meditation practice? My view is that we don't need to be too concerned about definitions and labels. Many people will happily describe the process either as mindfulness or meditation – or even mix the two together.

It's my experience that many mindfulness programmes such as mindfulness-based stress reduction (MBSR), while powerful as applied therapy, are rigid and over-medicalised if you are just starting out. It might all seem too complicated and counterintuitive.

It really isn't. Meditation is straightforward and simple. Our approach stems from ancient meditation and yoga science, particularly from teachings of the Bhagavad Gita and Patanjali's Yoga Sutras and Eight-Limb system. Our approach though is entirely non-secular.

We have shaped these powerful tried and tested human techniques for wellbeing, insight and happiness into simpler and more streamlined methods that link directly to daily experiences so that we can successfully meet with today's challenges.

Modern meditation techniques weave together timeless wisdom with contemporary insight and scientific research into the nature of wellbeing and happiness. The result is a powerful, easy-to-learn and straightforward series of life-changing and empowering meditation techniques, free from the dogma and rituals central to more traditional practices or the complicated clinically-applied self-examination of many mindfulness courses.

The goal of **mindfulness** practice is to train one's thoughts to be on the present moment. In **meditation** it's the same, however, the technique involves going beyond or underneath or even to the 'source' of thought itself. With practice we learn to maintain an experience of total absorption, in a state of **'pure awareness'** in which one is fully awake and operating in the world but from a deeper sense of who you are and what you can do. This is sometimes referred to as a **'unitive experience'**.

Knowing and unifying with this deeper state of consciousness, that Being part of you, is the agent of change. You will know it when you feel it!

3. Meditation is not what you think

Learning to dive into a formal, applied meditation has to be a step-by-step process. We make haste slowly. This is mainly because meditation practice is not an intellectual process. We can't think our way into meditation, we can only feel our way. This is important because what meditation does is nurture and enliven our insight and our intuition. That is our inner teacher, which is exactly what intuition means.

When learning to meditate perhaps the most important thing to consider is the way we approach it. Don't expect to feel a certain way, because that will take you out of the present. It will be an unfolding experience which is summarised below, and some of which you may already be familiar with:

1. You start with the notion that you are already genuinely and essentially fine in this particular moment. It may not feel like it but you are. You might even feel happy. Happiness or a sense of wellbeing is your default setting. And with practice you can uncover, access and nurture your innate and natural sense of wellbeing, anytime, anywhere.

2. You don't need to do anything differently or go anywhere in particular. Right here right now is where you make your start. You already have the tools required to access and nurture your own innate wellbeing and happiness. But you don't need to change or shape what is happening on the outside – the technique is going inside. And with practice, you begin to know a space of absolute, pure awareness.

3. All it requires is a simple shift of perspective and a change of attitude; it's just a moment away. Then you begin to notice

thoughts, emotions, experiences and actions are all just an ongoing process appearing and disappearing. With practice, it begins to dawn on you that what you thought was you, turns out not to be you at all. There's something more.

4. It is then that you begin to see and feel things differently. You notice you are waking up a little. Switching on to what is really happening, not what you think is happening. With practice you notice you are more in the flow of things, not expecting them to be different by constantly judging, intercepting, interfering or changing them. You begin to know that you don't need to hold on all the time. You can let go a little and just remain in your space of awareness in the centre of flow.

5. As you learn to let go, your anxiety, stress and fear dissolves. You begin to react differently, accepting and responding openly and without judgement to every moment-to-moment experience. You feel more connected to yourself, to others and to what you're doing. With practice, you begin to act with more creativity and insight.

6. A new and deep sense of peace and harmony with the world around you grows from the inside out. Your perspective expands. You remain intimately connected with your experience, fully present to the moment, but also a deeper awareness begins which says you are more than your experience. With practice, a knowing, effortless joy begins to emerge from an inner point of stillness in your Being, right in your day-to-day life of Doing.

7. This enables you to feel yourself as a sustained experience of flowing, creative, spacious awareness, which is different from

simply being aware. Nothing or no one can hold you back. You are free from that negativity which causes self judging, resisting, or trying to change experiences, feelings, emotions and reactions that arise. With practice, you begin to apply and utilise this inner flowing creative force of momentum and purpose. You seem to know what to do anytime, anywhere.

And in this moment you feel fine. You are happy. There is nothing to fear. Nothing to worry about. Right here there is no suffering.

You will notice that you will think about things differently, see things differently and do things differently. It's about letting go, not clinging to your ego-driven desire for reward or ownership of outcome. Activity performed this way becomes a full expression of who you really are and what you are for. Everyday life then will unfold as a creative, spontaneous, effortless, flow where every action feels intuitively right, meeting the needs of each moment.

We mostly live in a world shaped by mental chatter, which impacts on what we think, see and do. We give a lot of attention to that inner voice, forgetting that our real lives are unfolding around us right now.

The important point is that the voice in your head is useful. We are not in the process of switching off that voice. Not least because that would be impossible. But instead we are learning to change our relationship to it. With practice, we begin to notice that there is more going on inside us than we **thought**, or what we have been led to believe. When we manage to change our relationship to the voice, the conversation changes. Instead of the mind worrying and fretting over **what** to do, the mind **knows** what to do.

Firstly, we notice there is the 'process of thinking' that is associated with the day-to-day working of the mind. This is just that 'voice in our head', which is the continuous narrative of judgements, worries and self-criticisms.

Secondly, there is a pure or inner awareness. This is the awareness that recognises the voice in your head. Because awareness is constant and ever-present, it unfolds when one's attention is directed to the moment through meditation practice.

This shift is important. It's at the heart of what meditation practice is. It leads us to know a deeper awareness. A sense of being or self that is aware of and can 'see' your thinking or even your awareness. It's like being aware of being aware. The ultimate answer then to 'what does meditation feel like?' is it feels like FREEDOM! borne by the intuitive realisation that you are not your thoughts. You are something more. This knowledge is hugely liberating.

In the western world we have been mostly brought up in the Cartesian model of human reality: "I think, therefore I am". Modern meditators know this is not true and so will turn Descartes' conclusion around the other way – "I am, therefore I think."

In other words your innate sense of 'I am-ness' is primary, while your thoughts and ability to think is secondary. You are a conscious being without the need to think at all. Thinking will not provide you with the ultimate sense of who you are or where you are. You are more than thought. You are not your thoughts – they tend to get in the way.

4. Being Happy

We all want to find happiness and avoid suffering. It's just that many of us are looking in the wrong place.

The Dalai Lama tells us we are hard wired to be happy. That is our purpose, our default, our biological imperative. Happiness is what we are for.

"Human beings by nature want happiness and do not want suffering. With that feeling everyone tries to achieve happiness and tries to get rid of suffering, and everyone has the basic right to do this. In this way, all here are the same, whether rich or poor, educated or uneducated, Easterner or Westerner, believer or non-believer, and within believers whether Buddhist, Christian, Jewish, Muslim, and so on. Basically, from the viewpoint of real human value we are all the same."[1]

We often like to expand the term 'happiness' and use expressions such as satisfaction, contentment, creativity, joy and wellbeing. In the west, in Ancient Greece around 2600 BCE, Aristotle had a word for this felt sense of happiness: Eudaimonia.

---

1 His Holiness the Dalai Lama - *Kindness, Clarity, and Insight*

About the same time in the east, the ancient yogis went a little further and developed another expression: Sat Chit Ananda. Sat (sense of Self), Chit (consciousness), Ananda (bliss). In other words the felt sense of happiness and wellbeing was a default setting, which for ancient yogis could be explored and utilised. The emergence of meditation in the east developed as the primary tool providing access to and helping to shape a deeper insight into this conscious sense of self.

"Meditation... it's the bliss that comes with experiencing not mere happiness but complete satisfaction with the way things are. These are our moments of supreme quiet, total acceptance, and non-judgment. The wondrous intervals when we know we are in the right place doing precisely what we're supposed to be doing." [2]

I often begin my 'Introduction to Modern Meditation' course with this observation: "You are happy. You might not feel it but you are!"

It stimulates different reactions. Some know, some smile or laugh. While others say, "no Mick, I am not happy that's why I am here in your session!"

---

[2] *Essential Wisdom of the Bhagavad Gita - Ancient Truths for our Modern World. Jack Hawley. 2006*

Our problem is we tend to think happiness is a destination, something to be achieved at some point in the future when other parts of our life fall into line, such as that new look, a pay-rise, the latest smart phone, house, car, job, partner etc. We often assume that once we have achieved these things, that's what success looks like and we will become happy. In fact, research backed by ancient wisdom tells us that it's the other way around. We can't become happy, we can only be happy.

When we talk about 'happiness', we're not talking about a fake happiness that comes from some naïve sense of optimism or childish approach to the world. Nor does this innate happiness require faith or belief in anything. Instead, this happiness is real – it's authentic. It comes from the inside. Real happiness is always there and all you have to do is create the right context and conditions for it to grow.

Maybe then we need to expand our vocabulary and talk about life satisfaction and wellbeing. Some academics and positive psychologists argue that wellbeing, just as Jack Hawley said, can be measured in terms of our overall happiness or satisfaction with life. But perhaps more importantly wellbeing, happiness and personal flourishing is found in knowing that we make a difference and that our true capabilities and potential are maximised in a creative, fulfilling and useful way, which in turn nurtures that innate joy and satisfaction with the way things are.

This is the art of making happy work. And it's an aspect not lost in other fields of research looking at happiness in the modern world. For example, in their 'Wellbeing Manifesto for a Flourishing Society', The New Economics Foundation defined a sense of wellbeing emerging from the combination of two particular dimensions.

Firstly, there is what is referred to as a 'personal – wellbeing', which is what we might describe as 'Being' where one 'flows' through life in a fully engaged way, fulfilling inherent potential and purpose. An authentic experience of one's life having real meaning no matter what you do. Secondly, there is 'social – wellbeing', which we might call 'Doing' where what we do feels positive, useful and deeply connected to the wellbeing of ourselves, others, our community and society.

Here we see the same themes re-emerging again and again from timeless meditation science. The key to happiness, wellbeing and fulfilling one's potential in the world is simply a matter of connection and union between what we do and who we are. The **beanddo** meditation approach is to shape, direct and combine this powerful ancient science of **Being** into the modern world of **Doing**.

We search for happiness in external things because we feel there is something missing in our lives. This is why meditation exists, to help us understand and deal with this sense of lacking. In fact, many of the ancient teachings tell us it's always been like this. We all feel that there is something missing, that there is a void that needs to be filled. We all seem to know a feeling of incompleteness, one of dissatisfaction with how things are for us. In Buddhism this is called **Dukkha**, an important concept commonly translated as 'suffering', 'pain' or 'unsatisfactoriness'.

Key ancient texts such as the Bhagavad Gita are pretty clear that in order to fill this felt void and respond to that feeling of incompleteness, we mistakenly attach ourselves to external 'conditions' such as people, events, places and things, or what are referred to as 'sense objects'. This attachment often gets us into a lot of trouble:

"The Downward Spiral to one's ruin consists of the following process: brooding on (or merely thinking about) worldly attractions develops attachments to them. From attachments to sense objects come selfish desires. Thwarted desires cause anger to erupt. From anger arises delusion. This causes confusion of the mind and makes one forget the lessons of experience".[3]

These attachments are just another way of wanting to control stuff. We go deeper into confusion, the more we mentally and physically keep arranging external conditions into a pattern that we think will better meet our perceived needs, and that keep us happy and limit suffering and fear. But it never really works out. Because everything outside of us is in a constant state of flux and change. There are just too many countless and unknowable things to manage.

However, the feeling of dissatisfaction is also a useful one. It's a constant reminder that things could be different. It's almost as if we are 'invited' to want to know a deeper relationship to life by developing a better, more creative and inspiring relationship to our body and mind.

Let's cut to the chase.

---

3 *The Bhagavad Gita - A Walkthrough for Westerners. Translated by Jack Hawley*

How do we create that new relationship? We start by turning our attention to that voice in our head that we talked about earlier, but in a very specific way:

One of our problems is that we **confuse the voice in our head as ourselves.** We get caught up in it, identifying with the world being made in our head rather than what is really happening. It becomes the source of our pain and our suffering through sensations and emotions felt in the body.

All too often, it is an exhausting experience. So would it not be better to turn our attention to an alternative source of experience? A different sort of space to be and do. A mindset through which we can see the world just as it is, good or bad, without the constant, judging dialogue. To let go of wanting, expectation, scheming and worrying. Simply, to just be.

"The real voyage of discovery consists not in seeking new lands but seeing with new eyes."4

It's true. We don't need to go anywhere different or be anyone different. All we need to do is change our perspective on what is happening right in this moment. It's that simple. And that is the advantage of this modern meditation technique.

So the thing to do is learn to let go of your attachments, or better still change the way you see and respond to this world of change by cultivating a position of 'non-attachment'. This is the start of you shifting your perspective and going inward towards a place and space where there is only one thing to change – you!

---

4 *Marcel Proust*

This is the conscious shift inwards that empowers your own inner architect for change that I talked about in the introduction, because once you change you will find the world changes too.

After a while you will come to know a distinct inner space that seems to exist at the centre of you. An inner space around which your body, mind, events, actions and all other external conditions of your life seem to flow and circumnavigate.

After a while you will realise that this inner space is most definitely the real you. Your very own sense of being distinct and intimately connected to your body, mind or even your actions and environment. According to ancient wisdom, becoming conscious of knowing and inhabiting this Being space so that you know what it's like to be free, happy and vitalised is your only task while you are living on this planet.

5. What does modern meditation feel like?

When we are describing what meditation feels like it's often useful to describe what meditation isn't. It's likely that you will have heard or read some form of received definition of what meditation is, such as:

· Meditation is a form of relaxation.

· Meditation is a blissful trance state.

· Meditation is a form of self-hypnosis.

· Meditation clears away thoughts and feelings and makes the mind blank.

· Meditation is a form of mind control.

These mistaken assumptions rightly put many people off the practice.

While it's true that regular meditation practice will uncover a 'bliss' state and help you relax, this is just a by-product. The objective of meditation is to 'switch on' and raise our level of Being, not to fall into a trance or hypnotic state – that's no use to anyone.

So what is the meditation experience and what does it feel like? The chances are you have had a meditation experience very recently without even knowing.

Can you remember the last time your intuition blossomed, when you started to see things more clearly?

Can you remember when you were last in that perfect space.

When you were so involved in what you were doing in the moment that everything felt spontaneous, almost automatic? Did you notice that when you were in that state you weren't aware of your body, your surroundings or the people around you? Your awareness of yourself as a separate entity merged completely with the task you were performing.

Did you notice how time stopped? That thoughts about any imagined future outcome resulting from what you were doing didn't really matter. Expectation was replaced with just doing the task for its own sake. Did you also notice that every action and movement felt purposeful, smooth and effortless? Each action in each moment seemed to serve the next, and that you seemed to know what to do without being told.

Do you remember that you were calm, energised and maybe even a little excited? You were fully present. You were happy, infused with a sense of joy and wellbeing that emerged from somewhere inside.

Most people do. It's happening all the time.

We might miss it but it's there, moment-to-moment. It's just that most of us are distracted. This merging of action and awareness, or the joining of our being and our doing, brings a flowing, effortless quality to the task in hand. With meditation practice we learn to purposefully capture this experience and then apply it.

Like life, meditation is more about process than product or outcome. Sure, one can talk about the journey inwards, but that's more about how it feels. The point about learning to meditate is that we either get it straight away, or it can take some time.

Everyone is different. There are no set outcomes. There are no levels, no goals, no stages and no destination. It just is. All you need to do is decide to do it.

6. What are the benefits of meditation?

There are both measurable and not so measurable benefits to regular meditation practice. You will know them when they begin to unfold in your life. Old habits and outlooks will fall away.

This is the result of you noticing perhaps for the first time how your thinking is stuck day-to-day in a cycle of negativity, anger and judgement. From the start, remember if you can see it, it isn't you!

It will happen gradually but you will notice improvements in energy, health, performance, creativity and happiness. One of the very first experiences some of my students often report is a good night's sleep.

Generally you will notice:

Positive thinking - Cultivating your mind's natural desire for wanting to be in a good place.

Anxiety and stress-free living - Letting go of negative, painful thoughts and actions and learning to manage stressful situations and environments.

Self-esteem - Discovering who you are and what you can do to create a fulfilled and useful life for yourself and others.

Insight and clarity - Learning how to unlock and use your inner wisdom and knowledge every day.

Peace and wellbeing - Knowing how to stay centred, balanced and calm wherever you are, whatever you are doing.

Creativity and flow – Tapping into your innate creativity and letting it flow with joy into the world.

Happiness – Being happy, all of the time! A state of where the knotty problems of life just seem to fall away.

Warning!

There are, however, side effects you need to be aware of. With practice, you will notice changes in your behaviour and outlook leading to:

- Smiling and talking to strangers.
- Moments of joy and happiness for no apparent reason.
- Feelings of being calm and centred.
- Moments of insight and clarity.
- Increased energy, focus and sense of purpose.

Should you experience any of the above, keep practicing.

The objective of modern meditation practiced and taught at **beanddo** focuses on already being in a good place, rather than tackling being in a bad place. This is an important distinction, because working to enliven all of the positive resources we have will naturally bypass one's troubles and anxieties into a place where they will find it hard to get a grip. Stress reduction is something that happens naturally.

So do not think of modern meditation as something to fall back on when you are feeling challenged or troubled – or a way to close yourself off from the world. Instead, think of it as a way to know your deeper consciousness underneath your thinking. The real and essential you. Because this is the part of you that is never stressed or anxious. It is that part that knows things as they really are, leading to a greater and higher sense of reality, which in turn leads you to a fuller, more creative and vital state of being.

When we practice modern meditation we are not looking for comfort, joy or solace. In fact it's important to ensure we are not choosing to look for anything in particular, as this distracts the mind and pushes it back into our Doing field and into expectation. If we employ the techniques of modern meditation correctly, those benefits will come naturally.

Knowing your best self like this will give you a good idea of your strengths so you will build confidence to handle anything that life brings you. As we like to say in our classes, '**you can pick up yourself with your Self!**'

Remember: we are not in the process of switching off, but instead switching on.

Meditation is not a retreat from the world; rather, it's a vital component to making all activity conscious and creative. We do this by linking mind and body, thought and action, Being and Doing together.

7. How does modern meditation work?

Meditation is a simple, mental cognitive technique designed to promote a deeper shift of attention. This shift is often described as 'being aware of being aware', or 'paying attention to paying attention'.

We can answer the question, 'how does meditation work?' by looking back at 2600 years of practice. We start with Patanjali, sometimes referred to as the originator of modern yoga meditation practice. He devised the Yoga Sutras, which is what most of our contemporary practice is based on. The first four lines of the Yoga Sutras start with:

1. And now the teaching of yoga begins.

2. Yoga is the settling of the mind into silence.

3. When the mind has settled, we are established in our essential nature, which is unbounded Consciousness.

4. Our essential nature is usually overshadowed by the activity of the mind.[5]

The word 'now' is important. When Patanjali states that now it's time for yoga (here he is referring to the core science of yoga and its primary practice of meditation, not the physical postures of yoga you might be thinking of) he means right here, right now. Because it's only in the now that meditation works. Patanjali

---

5 *Effortless Being: The Yoga Sutras of Patanjali. Translated by Alistair Shearer*

tells us that once we learn to settle the mind and change our relationship to what is going on in our head, we begin to see things differently. We connect to our inner core, which previously had gone unnoticed because of all the mental noise and agitation.

Now compare Patanjali's first sutra with this insight made more recently.

"... if you just sit and observe, you will see how restless your mind is. If you try and calm it, it only makes it worse, but over time it does calm, and when it does, there's room to hear more subtle things - that's when your intuition starts to blossom and you start to see things more clearly and be in the present more. Your mind just slows down, and you see a tremendous expanse in the moment. You see so much more than you could see before. It's a discipline; you have to practice it."[6]

The similarities are striking. The conclusion is our mind is both an obstacle and a vehicle towards a deeper experience, perception and insight of ourselves and the world. If we learn to still the **thinking** mind, and as a consequence activate the

6 Steve Jobs, as quoted by biographer Walter Isaacson

knowing mind, we can look, see and know more clearly – and from that shift of perspective comes significant and profound change. We gain an experience and realise, if only for a moment or two, our essential nature.

The whole universe, everything being experienced right now by you, is defined by just two modes – your **inner life** and your **outer life**. In other words, your **Being** and your **Doing.**

There is nothing else.

Your experience is a matter of where and how you place your attention. It's nothing to do with what you think you see. It's what you actually see that counts.

When it comes to meditation practice, which is all about how you direct your attention, we can explain this in a different way. Our everyday attention is often determined and shaped by two different experiences. The first we might call a horizontal experience which is to do with the world, what we are doing and where we are. This is our outer experience of the day-to-day spatial and material world. It's a world of matter, space and time. It's where we operate all of the time. We can call it a field which contains all of our 'Doing'. It's an external, constantly changing spatial, physical and temporal experience where we find ourselves interacting with a multitude of passing events, objects, other people and places. We have a body, mind and senses which convey the experience of this 'Doing' field, even though most of 'what we think' is happening in the Doing field, it 'appears' pretty much in our head as we constantly analyse, judge and want to change and manage what is happening. This is the mental attachment to external things that we talked about earlier.

The other experience is what we might call a vertical one. This is where we cut through the horizontal into the here and now. To know this we need to see without judgement or analyse things as they are right now. This is an inner experience and it's to do with who we are at the core of us.

It's a deeper awareness of one's self, not determined by events in the outer Doing field, but they are connected. This is the essential nature referred to by Patanjali as an inner state as 'pure consciousness'. It's a field of unlimited insight, creativity, energy and joy underneath, inside or beyond action, events, thoughts and experience. This experience is 'felt' in the Doing field. This is the inner space discussed earlier, which exists before thinking, reacting and planning.

This inner self or the experience of it happens in our 'Being' field.

Our problem lies in the fact that we get attached more to the horizontal, the Doing, at the expense of Being. We are distracted by the noise, movement and colour of the Doing field. In fact we get so attached to it that we start to think that the Doing is ultimately who we are. We project our Being onto our Doing. This causes us to misunderstand experience, lose sight of reality and feel unbalanced and off-centre. We all intuitively know about this deeper experience and in many ways we long for it, which is why we often feel there is something missing in life; a deeper, more meaningful connection with something more fundamental about ourselves. We want to feel alive, but it's often the case that we don't fully engage with that absence until something goes wrong.

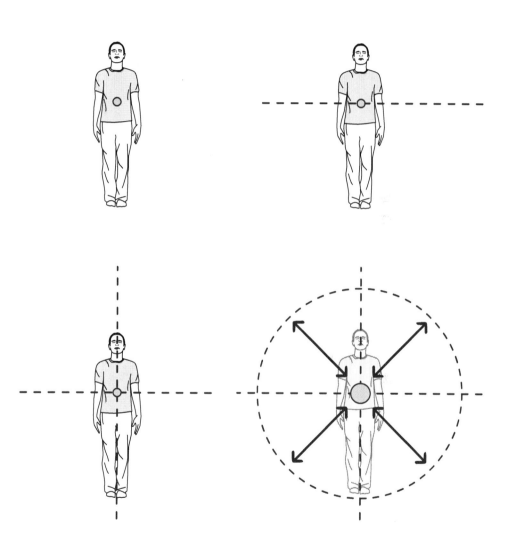

Fig 3. Horizontal and vertical experience. Merging your Being and Doing fields. Four parts.

1. We start with where you are right now. Or more accurately we start with your mind-body field or complex. Everything happens here. We don't need special equipment to get started other than a body that breathes, a nervous system that senses and a mind that is open.

2. We then start to direct our attention in a specific way towards our horizontal experience , or surface continually moving experience of doing. Your mind-body complex is an essential part of the Doing field in constant action. We begin to notice the link between directed attention and how we feel and sense.

3. With practice we then begin to expand our attention inwards. As this vertical experience crosses over the horizontal experience we begin to feel more present, centred in the moment through the mind-body field. The body begins to relax and the mind settles as the experience of things, just as they are in the here and now, build a sense of sustained present moment awareness.

4. Then after a while and with regular practice a shift begins to happen in the way we 'see' and perceive. Gradually at first but with practice done with intention. As we begin to 'watch' or 'observe' the events and experiences as 'objects' rising and falling in the Doing field, we begin to nurture an intuitive sense of inner spatial awareness or 'Being', which simply 'witnesses' the Doing field as it flows. Here we are beginning to open up and expand that inner consciousness, inwards and outwards.

We have forgotten how to make that connection, to intersect our horizontal experience with a vertical one — to Be and

Do together in the present. When we learn, with meditation practice, to focus attention on the intersection of the vertical and horizontal, it pinpoints a moment full of profound insight. Being and Doing merge into an experience of unified wholeness. You will feel that flow if only for a moment or two in whatever you are doing.

As you can see, meditation practice and its benefits are deeply relevant to you now. It's not about some guy with a long beard sitting for years in a cave in the Himalayas – it's about you! It's about how you assemble that piece of machinery, build that wall, write that report, prepare for that important presentation, run that race, design that product, sell that service, sing that song, play that instrument. More importantly it's about where you are, who you are and what you can do. Modern meditation will set you free. With practice you will find when you link to that inner stillness, that sense of Being as you go about your day, you will find the tools and resources to help you deal with that limiting inner critic, that sense of doubt, that persistent nagging feeling of anxiety in the pit of your stomach or that rush of stress and apprehension.

You can deal with those inner critical voices by uncovering and reconnecting not only with your innate sense of wellbeing and wholeness, but also potential and purpose. We explore this benefit more in part 2.

8. Being and Doing

When we achieve this shift towards Being through Doing we begin to experience a wholeness, a wellbeing, as we externalise our inner world (Being) into the outer world (Doing). The key to beanddo modern meditation is simplicity.

Our core algorithm to Making Happy Work is:

Happiness = being + doing - Interference

Ha = be + do - I

Being	your constant, unchanging inner world of consciousness and wellbeing.
Doing	your constantly changing outer world of action and reaction including your thoughts and emotions.
Interference	your thinking, judgement and mental expectation. The voice in your head.

When we master this union of **Being and Doing** we enter a flowing, highly-tuned, spontaneous, productive and creative state. In other words we are **Being** the action and not just **Doing** the action. We activate the algorithm through modern meditation. There are two distinct but interrelated techniques – practices and applications – that relate to your Being and Doing.

The formal practice relates to the Being field, which is cultivated through your formal sitting meditation practice. The application relates to the Doing field where you then make everything you do outside of your formal sitting practice into a meditation. Over time however, these two aspects will merge into one.

The practice – **BEING**

The purpose of this practice is to let go, stop, nurture attention inwards through the body and settle the mind from passing thoughts, emotions and distractions. To come into the present, no matter how fleetingly. After a while an engrossing sense of open awareness will develop from the inside out. This will feel like a space in which to just be and inhabit. The mind and body is perfectly tranquil and still but equally fully alive and alert.

To practice, one must retreat to a reasonably undisturbed place and sit, upright with intent. You must learn to observe without judgement or attachment to what is happening, as it happens.

We start with the body breathing and this is our way in as a foundational practice. From there we learn to not let the attention rest or be shaped by any particular conceptions, thoughts or feelings that arise in the mind, body or externally via the senses.

Total awareness is the result. An open, knowing intuitive sense of wholeness of just Being.

The application – **DOING**

The purpose of this practice is to develop the habit of applying the insight and sense of being developed through the sitting practice into one's day-to-day activities and actions.

Whatever one is doing, whether it is standing, walking, sitting or working, you apply your attention to the act and the doing of it and not on your relationship to it. So when one is Doing, you just observe the act of doing and remove any interference or attachment to it. You simply observe that there is standing, walking, sitting or working. It is just happening. There is no 'I am doing this', instead simply concentration on the act itself. As in our Being practice, we simply observe and witness passing action as it happens. After practice one begins to notice old habits and hindrances disappear. Fear and doubt are weakened and in their place grows confidence, creativity, satisfaction and flowing awareness.

With practice you essentially become an open receiver, a highly tuned receptor to your life. You will see that you can isolate and enhance the signal coming from the merging of your Being and Doing from all of the noise and interference.

This is the joy of Doing and it can be known right now. And it's a joy related to the moment right here, beyond knowledge, expectation or output and any intellectual analysis. This is wisdom through a direct experience of insight and intuition and once realised, you combine both and fully apply it in daily life. Then after a while you will develop a creative, skilful insight into the world and what you are doing. Your sense of purpose and potential expands.

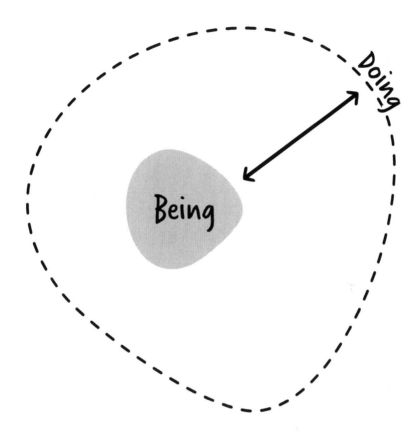

Fig 4. Connecting the Being and Doing fields

When we achieve this shift, balancing Being with Doing, we begin to experience a wholeness, a wellbeing as we externalise our inner world (Being) into the outer world (Doing). In other words we are **being** the action and not just **doing** the action.

Timeless teaching tells us that the best way to get through life, in fact to experience life fully, is to recognise these two experiences not as distinct and separate but as something connected. Instead, join them together into one **unified experience**, state or field. Our Being and Doing come together. This brings us to the very meaning of meditation as part of the wider teaching of yoga – to join, to unify, to 'yoke' together.

You'll find they are a good fit – they are designed to work together.

Modern meditation science calls this state the unified field. A place where the two different parts of us become one. A state of **non-duality**. And it's a meditation experience.

To create, manage, inhabit and apply this unified field requires simple modern meditation practiced little and often. We begin with a formal sitting practice and after a while the benefits you will notice evolve and impact during your daily routine. The unified field of experience, the characteristic of which no matter how fleeting, is wholeness, creativity, balance and happiness – or innate wellbeing. When you work towards intersecting the vertical and horizontal lines of your Being and Doing you find yourself feeling very different about who you are, where you are and what you are doing. You reconnect with your own sense of wellbeing, purpose and potential. In other words, the world changes and all you did was shift your attention.

This state of oneness is sometimes called 'flow' or 'optimum performance' in positive psychology. If you practice Transcendental Meditation this is what is what TM teachers mean by 'transcendence'. It's not just about sitting in meditation, it's about active engagement moment-by-moment. When you join your Being with your Doing you have pretty much nailed it.

Congratulations – welcome to the experience of real life!

Modern meditation is simply learning to be aware of what is happening both within and around us moment-to-moment. It's simple and easy because we learn to direct our attention and observe our body, mind and senses as they naturally do what they do, in constant motion interacting with the Doing field.

Learning to watch or observe the flow of what is going on without being immersed, distracted or wanting to change things is challenging. But it's worth it because that shift of perspective is what activates the deeper empowering benefits of meditation.

After a while you will notice that you can access that still, centred being part of you, which flows without impact or distraction. This leaves you to act, think and respond from a deeper source of inspiration, compassion, insight and creativity. With practice you will get the measure of this shift, which will then continue to promote the being part of you to reconnect and become part of your everyday doing. This is the art of making happy work. Then you flow through life revealing that the key to a happy, creative and purposeful life is not so much what you do through life but **how you live** through life.

9. Preparing to practice

Begin your practice without expectation. Meditation is not therapy but everything good you need will evolve and grow, and everything that you need to change, will eventually change.

To set this up we start by establishing a place to practice and then get the mind and body in that place. The techniques do not involve personal psychoanalysis, unpicking the nature of negative thoughts, feelings and anxieties. This is because we know that negativity will lift naturally and stress and anxiety will dissolve through the practice. You do not need to examine or theorise too much – just practice – in the knowledge that you already have all the resources you need for transformation.

Ancient meditation wisdom often refers to people who meditate as 'farmers', in that they are cultivating fields to allow good things to grow. It is your body and mind that is the ground being prepared:

"Any change into a new state of being is the result of the fullness of nature unfolding inherent potential.

But the apparent causes of a change do not in fact bring it about. They merely remove the obstacles to natural growth, as a farmer clears the ground for his crops".[7]

---

7 *Effortless Being: The Yoga Sutras of Patanjali. Translated by Alistair Shearer*

Your objective is to **tend and cultivate your deeper ground** of Being, to allow your own sense of resilience, insight and composure to grow. Be watchful, and over time you will get to learn the signs of how you are progressing.

Then you will know what we mean by **practicing to stay in a good place, rather than tackling being in a bad place.**

To begin with you will need to find a regular space for you to develop your formal sitting meditation practice. Some people like to establish a specific space to practice in.

The space you choose does not need to be completely silent. In fact, some occasional background noise such as passing traffic, aircraft or weather can be useful. Obtrusive, sudden noises such as phones, television or overheard conversations in adjoining spaces are not advisable. The mind is very easily drawn to the human voice and will try to understand what is being said. Unless you are listening to guided meditation, don't use earphones either.

You will know when a space feels right for you to practice in. The space need not be large. If you don't have access to a separate space then just a corner of a room will be fine. Good ventilation, some daylight and a view outside towards a garden, or up to the sky and passing clouds is ideal. You might want to light some incense or a scented candle. Have a small blanket handy to put around your shoulders or on your lap to make sure you stay warm.

Start by establishing the conditions for meditation such as the right posture. Often people will assume there is a 'correct' posture for meditation.

Yes and no.

The point is to be comfortable and upright. If the body is alert and present, the mind will follow. Learning to 'lean-in' to the posture reinforces the practice. As your practice develops, feelings about what is, and what is not comfortable, will not be an issue. Meditation is a full mind-body practice.

Bringing yourself into the correct position helps you to orientate to a place of notice. Think back to when you wanted to pay attention to something directly. Do you remember it being a whole mind-body experience, so that you orientated yourself to be still in one place and then directed attention so that for a moment you decided not to be distracted but fully connected to what you were doing? And it was an automatic action that you did. So now with meditation we're going to exploit that tendency and switch on our ability to notice, purposefully.

The two best postures are either sitting on a zafu (meditation cushion) legs bent with one leg in front of the other or sitting in a chair (ideally without arms) with the back straight and held up. The point of the zafu is that it will naturally tip the hips forward helping you sit upright. If you are using a chair you can also choose to use a cushion on the floor under your feet if you are unable to touch the floor and the back of the chair simultaneously.

Fig 5. The right meditation posture for you

Whatever position you choose, you need to ensure that you can remain reasonably still and upright for progressively longer periods in order to promote a mindful, ready alertness. The mind and body need to be held in a steady but relaxed state of awareness. Don't feel that in order to meditate successfully you need to master sitting crossed-legged on a cushion. I can sit for extended periods in this position only because I have had over 25 years of yoga asana practice. But if this is not comfortable for you, don't do it. Meditation can be practiced just as well in a simple chair with an upright back. After a while you will learn to switch on your meditation practice anywhere, anytime, so thoughts about the right sort of space, chair or cushion will not be an issue.

However, you shouldn't practice meditation lying down on your bed, yoga mat or sofa. You need to actively support the body so that you give both it and your mind ample opportunity to fully take part. This is what we mean by leaning into the practice. If you are lying down, you are giving over this role to whatever it is you're lying on. Similarly, when lying down it is very easy to fall asleep and you will not be supporting the spine and back correctly. Remember, we are attempting to cultivate a present moment awareness with things as they are at any given moment and that means the mind-body sitting ready with intention in meditation.

If you are using a chair, make sure to place both feet on the ground and remove your shoes. Place a yoga block or cushion under your feet if you can't touch the floor. Ensure that the lower spine is resting into the chair angle and back, but the upper spine self supporting. Pay particular attention to keeping the spine and body upright, but not held in tension – just relaxed and 'stacked' gently upright, with the chin tucked slightly downwards. Drop your shoulders away from the ears which will help to extend the upper spine and head.

To begin with you might have difficulty maintaining position. After a while the sitting position becomes uncomfortable or the body will slump. Watch out for this and regain your starting, upright position. At the start **you will need to do this often**. Don't worry too much about your altering position or moving during meditation practice – the important thing is to find what works best for you.

Learning meditation is similar to learning to relax. One will fall into it simply by the conscious act of doing it. It cannot be forced, just experienced and explored. It's important not to expect or desire a meditation experience but to just accept whatever comes through. It will take time and consistent practice.

As I have said so far, meditation is not a destination, it's an ongoing experience. This is achieved by learning to not try too hard. Thinking about doing, wanting to succeed, causes interference and directs us into Doing mode at the expense of our Being mode.

The result is a tension and distraction that develops from a mindset that's locked into 'trying' to do meditation. Similar to letting go, the idea of not trying too hard will be a difficult concept to grasp initially.

However, this shift and the benefit of letting go, of trying not to try, will come naturally if you let it. You will know when you have it. But also remember that it flows. It will come and go. An important aspect of establishing your practice is also intention setting. This is not to do with thinking about intended outcomes or specific acts of practice but simply with the intended act of doing it. Set yourself an intention that you will practice. That you are a modern meditator and the rest will follow. The joy and benefit of meditation is in the doing of it.

You might decide to meditate daily, for just five minutes at a time. Regularity is important. Remember you are a farmer. All you are doing is planting seeds, which you cultivate, every day. It will grow in time, in its own way, to enrich life. After a while you can then extend your sitting practice. Aim for 20 minutes twice a day, once before breakfast and then before your evening meal. There are plenty of meditation timer apps you can download to your smartphone. A word of warning though: if you use your phone, resist looking at it just before or after your practice! You will be amazed how putting that time aside is easier than you think. After a while you will start to look forward to your practice.

Sometimes you can anchor the focused and relaxed experience by setting an intention in each practice session. This will help to strengthen the focus and engagement and set a good potential energy for your practice.

An intention I often use in class is:

"I am exactly where I planned to be
I am doing exactly what I planned to do
In this moment there is nowhere else to be
There is nothing else to do
This is it
I am here
Only now is real."

10. Everything that isn't you

Every meditation technique uses a meditation object: something to direct your attention towards in a particular way. You may have read about some meditation techniques that use a mentally repeated word or phrase called a mantra. You may have seen meditators passing a string beads through their fingers called a mala. What makes the **beanddo** meditation different and perhaps more attuned to where you are is that the meditation object we use is readily available – you and your moment-to-moment experience.

Basically, a meditation object is everything that isn't you. Everything that is arising in your Doing field. It can be sensation, breathing, thought, action, feeling, an event etc.

To use and know an object for meditation means to experience whatever it is with bare, non-verbal awareness. You merely register the sensation with impartial attention, without identifying, judging or describing it. You don't have to comment on the experience of the object or try to shape it in anyway. We are only interested in the event, as a non-attached observer and receptor of the experience.

All meditation objects arise out of the Doing field. In meditation we learn to watch, observe and witness each object as it rises and falls in awareness. For example, if you use the body breathing as a meditation object, it's not the quality or nature of breathing that we are interested in, it's just the process of the body breathing as a flowing experience in the Doing field.

The key is to know and let go.

As you nurture your facility for non-judgemental observation, your awareness builds through your ability to be non-attached. This process is also known as witnessing. These are core meditation skills which will underpin the shift towards being aware of being aware, or that paying attention to paying attention.

Over time you can gradually introduce different meditation objects. To create that open awareness or witnessing, you mentally label each object as it appears and disappears. Don't be overwhelmed by this; simply know that it will take practice.

All objects are experienced. They are divided into two types:

1. **Material object** refers to a sense, impression, colour, sound, odour, tactile sensation, action (including bodily movement) or flavour.

2. **Mental object** refers to such things as pleasant or unpleasant feelings, desire, anxiety, peacefulness, anger, thought and so on.

Thus, an object is something that is **known** by the mind (something to be aware of) in the present moment. In meditation this shift happens when you learn to watch, observe or witness. You become the **knower** that is **knowing it** without judgement as a non-attached witness or observer. We are the observer, observing the body and mind experience objects as they flow. We use our current context and conditions as our starting point to move inwards linking Doing to Being. Remember when I talked earlier about that feeling of inner space around which everything flows? Now we see how that inner space of Being links to the outer space of Doing. When you cultivate your awareness of witnessing you suddenly become highly tuned to what is happening and the process by which it all happens.

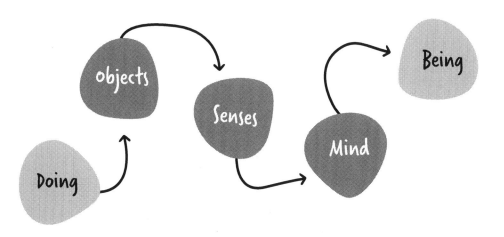

Fig 6. The path through which you can connect Doing with Being

Doing – The flow of our day-to-day actions, events and encounters. In summary, everything that isn't YOU!

Objects – Passing phenomena of experience from the world arising in the mind. In summary, everything that isn't YOU!

Sensing – All of those objects that are experienced through the senses, in the mind and body. In summary, everything that isn't YOU!

Mind – The senses convey object impressions to the mind, which then process all those impressions. In summary, everything that isn't YOU!

Being – Meditation starts with, but then goes beyond, objects, senses and the mind, diving into pure consciousness that is the recipient and witness of all of this. Ultimately, the question of effective meditation comes down to the single question, "Who is doing the experiencing?" The answer is YOU, as pure conscious awareness. You are BEING!

When we come to understand this as a practice and managed experience, we see that it works as a continuous feedback loop, allowing us to flow creatively with purpose in everything we do.

When we sit to practice we utilise the basic palette of meditation objects. This next diagram illustrates how our practice develops from sitting still to an active meditation applied to daily life.

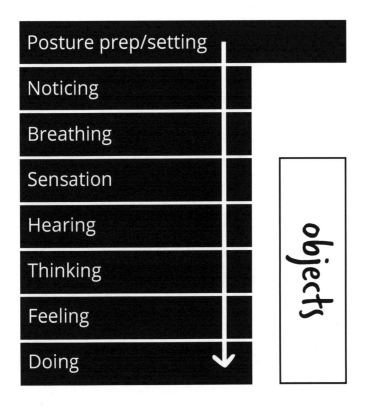

Fig 7. Palette of meditation objects. You can use them one at a time or mix them up.

As you can see there are seven basic meditation objects. In reality of course, there are countless objects. Meaning the whole world is a chance to practice meditation.

Once we establish our posture we begin with a short 'Noticing' practice. This is designed to draw our attention inwards, build mind and body awareness as a preparation to formal practice. Then we cultivate that open, receptive, witnessing object-by-object, until we learn to move our meditation - nurtured awareness from simply sitting still, towards doing what we do.

Having covered some of the core components of meditation and the reason why we need to go inwards, we now are ready to practice. In Part Two we will explore our original circular map in more detail. Our intention now is to use the tools and insights explored in Part One, visit each location and hopefully the journey will reveal to you, moment-by-moment, a brighter, newer world in which you can **be different and do differently.**

PART TWO

1. Navigating the Map

So let's make a start.

We begin by just **being** ourselves, where we are and what we're **doing** right now. This is the core of our practice, joining together our Being and Doing.

Remember in Part One I described our horizontal (Doing) and vertical (Being) experience and how we spend our time shuttling between these two fields, but mostly advancing outwards.

Now through meditation we can begin to unite and balance the two together by residing in our inner field of Being, while simultaneously participating in the outer field of Doing. After a while we become more and more alive to ourselves, to others and to the world around us. We meet ourselves and we meet the world by bringing that inner quality to the outer world.

To do that we return to our original map and follow it in more detail. Each element is designed to incrementally explore not only the practice of meditation but also the likely outputs and experiences. Each location is an invitation to go deeper into the meditation experience. This is our starting point. With practice, meditation can become an active part of daily life, making everything we do a meditation.

It's obviously impossible to divide these parts neatly. They merely serve as a structure in which to observe, explore and experience relevant and personal meditation outputs. Don't feel these are progressive stages. They are simply different aspects of the same overall intention. With practice, you will intuitively know how you move from one to the other until they all weave together into one unified field of practice.

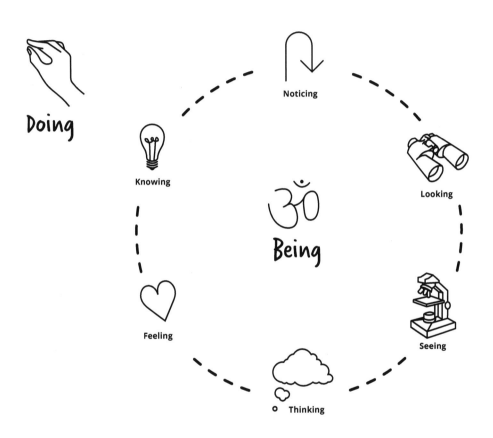

Doing

Noticing

Knowing

Looking

Being

Feeling

Seeing

Thinking

Fig 8. A more detailed navigation of the map.

Noticing

Fig 9. Noticing

This first part is designed to establish core principles about what meditation is (and isn't) and what the experience might be. The emphasis is on helping you to relax, let go and redirect your attention 180 degrees inward. The idea is to become familiar with different and probably underused cognitive and awareness skills, to stop and then notice what is happening in the present moment. This shift of perspective is a prelude to meditation practice. It might feel like a familiar experience or it may be new. The point is the experience now will be the result of a voluntary practice and that might be new to you. Noticing techniques include linking the mind and body, allied with intention setting, relaxation and body awareness.

Looking

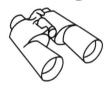

Fig 10. Looking

From learning to stop and notice, this second section is then designed to help you reinforce and deepen new found skills that have emerged through the Noticing technique. Looking, in this regard, entails learning to direct attention towards a particular object. The objective is to help you develop new skills that will enable you to switch on awareness to the mind–body complex at will. This shift of attention will be new, tentative and sporadic to begin with but with practice one can look inward with purpose.

Seeing

Fig 11. Seeing

Having developed the ability to direct attention, this seeing part is about learning to manage, maintain and shape attention in a particular way towards experience. Seeing now involves a purposeful exploration, combined with a very particular method of observation (non-attachment or witnessing). As one progresses, it is clear that a different experience of oneself can be seen, beyond the previously accepted, and obscuring assumptions, judgement and feelings. Seeing involves lifting away from the limiting, self-created identification of the Doing field towards Being. Awareness builds and the possibility of seeing more expands.

Thinking

Fig 12. Thinking

As your ability to see is refined, you will then begin to realise that thoughts too can be observed as a passing phenomena and therefore a meditation object. This is a major shift of perspective. The realisation that you are not your thoughts, or the thinking process, and that it's possible to loosen, disengage and go behind or beyond the voice in one's head to a deeper experience of oneself, is powerful and liberating.

Feeling

Fig 13. Feeling

As we begin to develop the skills to observe our thinking, we begin to notice how feelings in the mind and body are deeply connected to different types of thought and our reaction to them. With practice, we begin to observe and then create a space dissociated from our thinking and how it makes us feel. We can then recognise and tackle directly negative emotions, assumptions, attitudes and beliefs that we have collected over time.

Knowing

Fig 14. Knowing

As we liberate ourselves from the self-created bubble of our negative thinking and feelings, a deeper experience of ourselves and the day-to-day world is possible. At this stage, we begin to explore how meditation practice uncovers and nurtures a deeper knowing intuition. Your new meditation skills of witnessing and non-attachment are key.

Being

Fig 15. Being

Here we bring the meditation practice to its core output. The ability to stay present with a felt sense of Being through a sustained present -moment awareness. The intention is to feel that the sense of being is beyond any limited sense of mind-body ego - identity. Being uncovers a 'naturally arising' innate wisdom which puts us in the flow of things, ready for effective Doing.

Doing

And so this last part is all about integration —
merging Being and Doing. Here, the emphasis
is on how to apply the insight gained from
meditation (Being) into one's daily activity
(Doing). This is the art of making happy work.

Fig 16. Doing

All of these parts are woven together into a whole, cultivating
an attentive, non-judgemental awareness of one's experience
moment-to-moment. We start by focusing on the body, then
the breath, then the wider field of experience. With practice you
develop an intuitive, receptive, spontaneous awareness that
reveals everything, having deep and rich content fused with a
sense of purposefulness. Nothing is wasted. Every experience
is useful and our relationship changes are simply shifts in
perspective. We see all action, thoughts and experience flow
naturally and rise up into our awareness. We are separate to our
experiences but also deeply connected to what is happening; we
are both observer and the participant, the Being and Doing.

This is the wholeness created when we make that shift and
switch over from the egocentric 'I, me and mine'. We are then
free to respond perfectly to each situation we find ourselves in
and with that sense of harmony comes a flow of innate joy in the
field of our mind and body.

So before we dive in I will remind you to not try too hard. We
get used to applying lots of effort to achieve things in life. The
modern meditation journey is completely the opposite — it is an
effortless practice. The action of letting go, combined with the
right balance of concentration and relaxation.

We cannot force it, instead we let it come.

2. Noticing

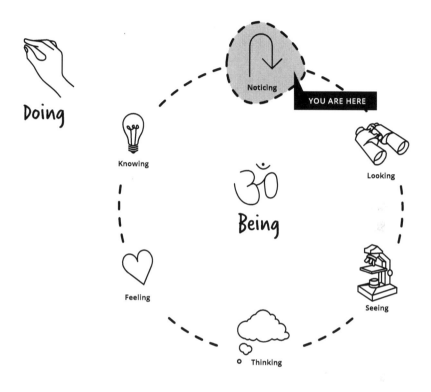

Doing

Knowing

Being

Looking

Feeling

Seeing

Thinking

Noticing

YOU ARE HERE

Fig 17. Noticing. Where you can discover how to direct attention and change perspective.

We start with the body.
All good meditation practice starts with the body.

If you go to a beginner's meditation class and your teacher
instructs you to visualise yourself standing on a mountain top,
ask for a refund. There is a place for visualisation but if you want
to do meditation properly, it's not the ideal starting point.
In order for meditation to work as a life-enhancing technique,

it has to start with real life in the first place. It has to have the merging of Being and Doing as its essential task, fusing the sense of Self with our experience of, and interaction with, the world.

Essentially, the objective of all meditation is **integration or union**. It strengthens our experiences of being in the world as it is. It enhances our sense of reality, who we are and more importantly what we can do. Meditation is not about creating fantasy worlds for us to inhabit. We start right here, right now with things as they are, not from some other imagined place.

We begin with the body, because the body is the threshold to our way in. It's both the map and the territory, directing our attention 180 degrees inward.

Noticing will provide you with a good platform from which to work. In my experience as a meditation teacher, the Noticing technique may appear challenging to some or very simple to others. It doesn't really matter which camp you fall into, the important thing is to not skip this first stage — instead, just get comfortable with learning to focus, directing your attention and knowing the deeper felt sense of awareness that this Noticing will cultivate.

To get started all we need to do is sit up and take notice.

This may sound easy, but think back: when can you honestly say you stopped, became still and fully directed your attention via the mind and body to what is happening, as it's happening — before becoming distracted by something else?
If we say meditation is simply **sustained present moment awareness**, then learning to stop and take notice is a fundamental meditation skill to build from.

We are going to learn how to direct attention and hold it where you need it to be in a very specific way, rather than allowing your attention to be taken away by something that is just passing.

This shift in how to pay attention is our way into meditation practice. The noticing process helps to build awareness; this is different from thinking. Even though you are directing your attention with purpose, the emphasis is on feeling rather than analysing. The point is to not define or describe, just feel. Again, this will help nurture the key meditation skill of non-attachment, which is learning to not judge, but just know and allow things to be just as they are. This is a skill which will naturally come with regular practice.

Noticing is a great prelude to your meditation practice. It will relax the body from the inside out, help you to settle inwards and bring you into the moment, even if only for a short time. You will notice that the practice also begins to prepare you for new and different experiences that will come through your deeper meditation practice. You will find you can sit still after all and you can focus the mind. You discover that you have a choice; you have all the resources and talents you could ever need to be different and do differently.

After a while you begin to notice that being able to sit still for meditation involves more than just the body. It's a mind thing too, as they combine together to hold you in the moment. Being able to align the mind-body requires the development of awareness. The Noticing practice is just that. We bring our attention inwards, towards an inner field of mind-body connectivity.

What does Noticing do?

Noticing is our way in, as it's designed to orientate us towards some of the deeper skills required for meditation, such as being open, centred and attuned to experiences in a particular way, as different sensations flow moment-by-moment. Noticing will help you to strengthen attention, concentration and nurture your deeper ability to be aware. It's a simple technique but it requires regular practice.

For the Noticing practice we employ something called body sensing. This is a simple body scanning technique but importantly undertaken in an upright, seated position. It might feel challenging at first but with practice, body sensing will help you to establish very quickly a sense of grounding, relaxation and calmness. Body sensing will help you feel embodied, whole and very present and will help you refine and sharpen your senses. Your perception of what is happening in the moment and how you respond to it changes — you learn to notice.

Moving away from the thinking mind

The Noticing technique is designed to reveal what it feels like to sense, notice, know and be aware, as opposed to thinking and critically-judging an experience which will disconnect and separate you. The reason we want to develop noticing and body sensing is that we are bringing our attention into something that is always present — you, or more accurately, your body.

Your body is always in the here and now.

All sensations and feelings in the body are rising and falling moment-to-moment. When we learn to sense those experiences

69

in the body we are connecting deeply to each moment, as every sensation passes or is sustained.

This in turn activates your body's natural relaxation response. Being present to everything automatically turns down your natural in-built negativity bias that is responsible for the fight, flight or freeze response.

Recent neuroscience research is revealing exactly what is happening in our mind and body as we practce meditation. Research shows that the deep relaxation that comes from body sensing will strengthen neural pathways and connections in the brain. You will notice this as your capacity to experience body sensing becomes deeper, easier and more instantaneous.

Be mindful that up until this point you have been directing your attention mostly outward. Now is the time to slow down, relax and guide your attention 180 degrees into the body.

The point is to take part and 'Notice' where you are and what you are doing in this moment. Be with yourself, without thinking you need to be somewhere else, doing something else.

Noticing Meditation
Practice: Sensing the hands

- Sit on a chair with a backrest.

- Just settle in for the moment. Be comfortable. Relax.

- Feel your body in the chair. Feel its position, its shape, its posture as it sits. Remember your body and sitting are in the Doing field. The body is sitting for you.

- Feel your back on the chair, your feet on the floor. Feel your hands resting in front of you.

- Place the backs of your hands onto your upper thighs. Hands open and fingers relaxed. Let the arms relax, falling into your lap. Let them rest and hang.

- With the eyes closed (or with a soft gaze), bring your attention to the fingers of your left hand.

- If at first you are unable to feel the fingers, just move them slightly so you can locate them mentally.

- Just feel them with your attention. Be aware of them. Don't think about the left hand, just be aware of it.

- After a while, you may be able to feel a gentle vibrancy. A subtle humming or buzzing in the fingers. When you notice, stay with it. Notice how your awareness of the radiant vibrancy is linked to your attention and how it's being directed.

- Notice how the depth and intensity of vibrancy is linked to your attention.

- It might come and go. It might have a wave-like form. Just stay with whatever you are feeling. It's fine as it is.

- Now let's see if you can widen and expand the sensation. Maintain the feeling in your fingers but now allow the radiant sensation to flow into the palm. Then into the back of the hand and then maybe the wrist. Now without letting go of the sensation in your left hand, add the right hand too.

- Now we are feeling it in both hands. Stay with it.

- Both hands are deeply linked to your attention.

- Again notice the vibrancy. The connection. Moment-by-moment we are connecting to the body. The mind and body, just for a moment, coming together.

It's here too that you might want to add your intention, or setting of focus, so that you can reinforce the type of mindset we talked about earlier.

Coming out of your Noticing practice

- Gently flex your fingers and toes

- Gently blink open your eyes. Allow the light to come in

- Avoid looking at anything in particular

- Now stretch if you need to

- Come back into the space

- Sit quietly for a moment. Don't rush

So what's happening?

You may have noticed that it was challenging trying to focus on both hands simultaneously. You may have felt the radiant sensation flow from one hand to the other, acting like a wave moving backwards and forwards. Sometimes the left hand was more apparent and then the right, or maybe the other way around. Maybe also the sensation disappeared or you lost track of it. Don't worry if that happened, because that's the whole point.

Firstly, when we try to direct our attention to two separate areas we notice our cognitive capacity and facility expands naturally from a singular, directed attention to a broader open awareness. With practice, you can actually feel this shift happen. So when we add other destinations for focus, the awareness will expand accordingly as directed attention begins to fall back.

As you begin to add more focal points, they operate like little orientation markers or coordinates around which your awareness space grows. For example, with practice you may wish to add toes too. Then expand into feet, hands, arms, legs and so on until you feel the whole body. With practice, you begin to create a space of pure awareness through which your meditation practice will evolve and grow.

Secondly, the radiant sensation you are feeling is the mind–body field itself and the vibrancy is the result of your directed connection to this field. You are simultaneously witnessing and orchestrating the ongoing connecting conversation between mind and body. If you begin to notice the vibrancy reduce or disappear it's only because your attention has wandered away. This is useful.

Staying with the vibrancy sensation is a great tool for keeping our attention where we need it — and the longer and deeper the focus, the more sustained the sensation. We make it happen and we keep that feedback loop going. We are focusing on the sensation just as it is without thinking about it. This is a great practice because when we begin to sense the body this way we are welcoming things just as they are, not as you want them to be. We are happy to be with the experience just as it is, as it flows and moves around the body.

You may have noticed a deeper sense of relaxation appear to rise up from the inside, rather than coming at you from the outside. Even just sensing the hands and maintaining that sensation initiates the body's sense of being present, still and grounded. The source of profound relaxation comes from simply being in the here and now.

Next steps

The point of the Noticing exercise is to know what it feels like to be totally present, even if only for a short moment or two. The point is your body is always in the here and now, as is your breath. For example you can't say, "I did far too much breathing at the weekend, so I won't breathe again until Friday." It's impossible. And the same goes for your body. It's yours 24-7, whether you like it or not!

Through practice, we can build the capacity to be present and stay present. We notice things begin to change; we realise that being present moment-to-moment is linked to attention, and in particular, how you direct attention and sustain it without effort.

We notice too that experience is ever-changing, it comes and goes. Sensation will arise and then pass. We also notice that aligning the mind-body to the moment directly links to what you're doing; Noticing begins to engage the body's natural relaxation response. We begin to notice new experiences such as feeling balanced, whole, connected, eased and grounded. These experiences seem to grow up from the inside, having very little to do with what's happening on the outside.

You may even begin to notice that there's an inner experience of spaciousness and lightness that comes from increased and improved awareness, and that you have some control over the shape, design and experience of this new inner space. You can build it. You are conscious of it, and if that space feels familiar, it's because it is. Because it's you. It's the beginning of knowing your own field of Being. Maybe you've also noticed for the first time that you are capable of changing how you feel. You can make a positive intervention into your mind-body field and unlock your natural sense of wellbeing moment-to-moment.

With practice, feeling the mind-body as a radiant sensation
of energy flowing through your day will become easier. You
will notice your breath change, your mind settle and your body
becoming open, spacious and light. Movement becomes effortless
and you begin to rest in a stillness, which can be switched on by
you throughout the day. So instead of being swept away by Doing,
you can anchor yourself into your Being through Noticing.

We mentioned at the beginning of this section that learning to
master the Noticing technique of body sensing is a prelude to
formal meditation practice. As you begin to sit for meditation,
always start with a short Noticing routine; with practice, this
technique will naturally compress and shorten as your ability to
engage and expand your awareness deepens. With practice, you
can switch on body sensing, almost instantaneously, allowing
you very quickly to move into your formal meditation practice.
You may want to start with the hands and feet to begin with, then
move very quickly into knowing and sensing the whole body.

Noticing is both a realisation and acknowledgement that you are
present and ready to meditate — that then becomes your way in.

But Noticing can also be employed as a distinct practice
throughout the day. Practice Noticing frequently, ideally every
day, in short bursts. Try Noticing while you're reading, working
at your desk, sitting in meetings, waiting for the train, while
on the train, walking and so on. As your mental and cognitive
capacity grows, Noticing will get easier and easier. It will become
effortless. This enables you to stay relaxed and connected to what
is happening, allowing you to experience your own wellbeing, no
matter what.

3. Looking

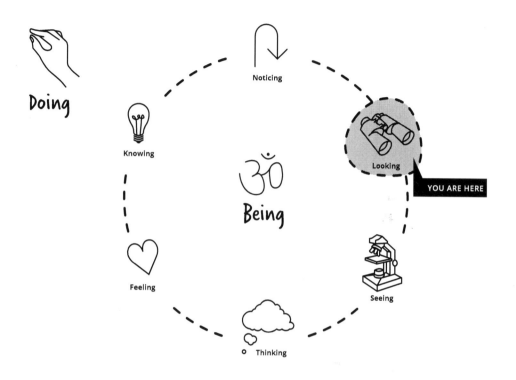

Fig 18. Looking. Where you can discover how to fine tune your directed attention.

Now we are ready to move towards the next space on our map – Looking, but with our eyes closed as we explore our first formal meditation practice.

Looking is designed to help you reinforce and strengthen the new-found skills that have emerged through the Noticing technique. Looking, in this regard, entails learning to direct attention towards a particular event or moment that is happening in the Doing field. If Noticing is about learning to stop and nurture a space of awareness, then Looking is directing

attention purposefully towards a moment, event or experience that arises within that space — or even the space itself.
The whole process of meditation is exactly that: a **process**, which is why we can make anything we **do** and everything we experience a meditation practice. It will take time and consistent practice. Learning to let go is the key. You will know when you have it.

Setting up base camp

In this next practice we will be learning to simply look at the breath. I call this base camp, as it's a place to come back to, but also a place to venture out from. We will view the breath as our first meditation object. Remember, all objects exist and flow in your Doing field. If you can see it, touch it, hear it, feel it or taste it, it isn't you. So your body breathing for you is happening inside your Doing field – you are simply an observing participant.

In this first practice you will observe the natural flow of inhalation and exhalation as the body breathes for you. The letting go aspect is that you do not interfere with the breath in any way — you simply observe and let the breath just be as it is from one moment to the next. We are just observing (Looking) towards the breathing action in the Doing field without judgement or expectation.

In Looking, our aim is to build a sense of connective space between you and what is happening. We cultivate one of meditation's core skills — non-attachment — and we do this by ensuring what is happening is something distinct and separate from you, but also at the same time something you participate in and create. **We do this by looking in a special way.**

How do we look in a special way?

We start by settling inwards. Remember: we are learning to orientate our attention and shift our perspective. It's less about effort and more about a gentle and passive witnessing on what is happening moment-by-moment.

You don't want to grab things as they appear; you want to let things come to you. Notice them as they arise in a receptive way, rather than reaching out actively. It's a passive looking rather than proactive seeing and understanding. We need to allow experience to come to you rather than you going out to the experience — this is how you learn to direct attention inwards.

Your default negativity bias is always scanning outwards with a plan to judge and assume. This is so that your nervous system can react with either fight or flight in response to something that might happen. Simply sitting and allowing the experience to come as it is, without a built-in preconceived plan of what might happen or has happened, subtly turns down your negativity bias and thus mental activity. When you are in the present, right here, right now there is nothing that wants to hurt you and there is nothing to fear.

Meditation object – Breathing

Many people think 'oh yes, meditation — that's to do with breathing isn't it?'

It isn't.

In fact, it's not really about breathing at all. It's just that breathing, or a body that breathes for you, is a useful foundation on which you can build and support your practice.

As the awareness begins to build we are going to see if we can direct attention and look towards a specific moment or meditation object. In this case it's the breath. The other thing to remember is: it's not you breathing!

In physical asana yoga practice we spend time developing breath consciousness and control. We practice shaping, changing and managing the breath, it's flow, rhythm and depth. A conscious breath changes everything. For yoga asana practice, breathing is the glue that binds action, body and mind together. In meditation practice, the breath is also useful, but unlike physical yoga there is no intention to manipulate the breath. We simply learn to observe the body breathing, as it happens.

With practice, we are going to shift from conscious breathing to being conscious of the breath. These are two entirely different things and so this is an important little shift. It is your first meditation challenge as we begin to meditate to shift our perspective. We are learning to simply look at the body breathing without expectation or critical analysis.

Building breath awareness

Many people are hardly aware of their breath at all.

Learning to direct attention to the breath without interfering with it means we have to know that it's working. We have to build an awareness of the body breathing. Just in the same way that noticing builds present moment awareness through body sensing, we are now going to deepen our practice by using the breath. We are not looking to shape or manipulate the breath.

There are four aspects:

1. Breathe through the nose, not through the mouth.

2. Breathe from the abdomen if possible and feel the body rise and fall as it inhales and exhales.

3. Understand that your breath, as the mind and body relaxes, will come in four natural interconnected parts. There is the inhalation, a momentary pause of retention (sometimes almost imperceptible), the exhalation, then a momentary pause before the lungs fill again.

4. Adopting an alert but relaxed upright meditation position will help you observe all of the above.

At first, when your attention is directed to the body breathing, you may find it difficult to not interfere with the process. You might find that you get in the way of the process by interfering such as:

-   Trying to force or shape the breath as you watch. This causes tension in the body.

-   Thinking 'should all the breaths be the same, am I doing it right?' This causes judgement and expectation.

To get the technique right we employ the **beanddo** algorithm of watching while not interfering, trying to disengage and let go from what is happening. After a while you will get it with practice. The intention here is to simply be aware and open to every passing phenomena as it rises and passes into and out of awareness. We are happy to invite and welcome experience but we are in receiving mode only. We will try not to process or shape what we experience or identify with it in any way. Eventually, with practice, a spacious, still awareness unfolds.

Adding breathing as a meditation object

We do this by looking at the body breathing. In Part One I introduced our basic pallet of meditation objects, from Noticing to Doing. To create and use a meditation object we have to learn the art of 'labelling'. In other words, simply observing mentally without attachment or expectation linked to what is happening in that moment. Observing without attachment or judgement is key to meditation and 'looking in a special way'.

To use the body breathing as a meditation object we simply watch the body breathe by mentally noting 'rising' as the body breathes in and 'falling' as the body breathes out. Nothing else is needed. Don't worry if this seems too hard, it really isn't. Sometimes you might forget what you are doing altogether as the mind wanders. In many cases that is the whole point. If you notice that has happened (and it will happen countless times) just bring your attention back to looking at and labelling the breath. This is why I call this practice 'Base Camp'.

Practice: Breathing meditation
Preparation

· Start by getting comfortable.

· Place feet flat on the floor, hip width apart, toes pointing forward.

· Make sure that the lower back is gently supported by the

angle of the chair, with the upper back away from the chair's backrest.

- Place the hands into cosmic mudra.

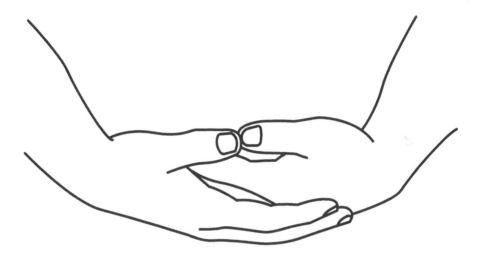

Fig 19. Cosmic mudra hand position

- Gently lift the crown of the head upwards towards the ceiling (a gentle elevation of the spine).

- Allow the chin to drop just a little toward the chest so that the face is forward.

- Close the eyes softly. Close the mouth softly and breathe through the nose.

- Then cultivate an open, relaxed mindset. Minimum effort is required, although concentration is a must.

Practice

- Just settle into the moment. Be comfortable. Relax.

- Feel your body in the chair. Feel its position, its shape, its posture as it sits for you.

- Feel your back on the chair, your feet on the floor. Feel your hands resting in front of you. Your arms falling into your lap. Let them rest and hang. Feel the hands and thumbs resting against each other.

- Again begin with a short Noticing exercise — feel the fingers, feel the hands, feel the toes, feel the feet...

- After a while you will feel a gentle vibrancy. A subtle humming or buzzing sensation. Stay with it.

- Draw your awareness/attention of that feeling upwards through the whole body, don't worry about areas that feel blocked or restricted. This is normal, just go where your mind-body lets you.

- When you Notice, stay with it. Notice how your awareness of the vibrancy is linked to your attention.

- Just stay with that experience for a moment or two.

- Now we begin to focus on breathing.

- But you are not breathing. Your body is breathing for you.

- Direct your attention to the abdomen. Find the point that seems clearest to you. Do not actually look, just feel it.

- As you breathe in notice the abdomen expanding; as you breathe out, it contracts.

- The sensation is subtle. As you relax, the breath softens and shallows.

- Don't try and change this in any way. Just let the body breathe for you.

- As the abdomen rises, observe the motion from beginning to end with your mind.

- When the abdomen falls, do the same. Just keep observing the rising and falling moments.

- Just know each event/moment without judging or identifying with them.

- They are just happening. You are just watching.

- The body is breathing for you.

- We are not interested in the quality, depth and feeling of the breath. Just the moment as a raw experience.

- To help with this we are going to mentally label each breath event/moment as a raw passing experience, just as it is.

- We call these events/moments 'objects'.

- When the body breathes in, label the experience 'rising'.

- When the body breathes out, label the experience 'falling'.

- Rising... falling...

- Rising... falling...

- As you do the practice, restrict your attention to what is occurring in the immediate present moment.

- Don't think about the past or future — don't think about anything at all.

- Let go of worries, concerns and memories.

- Just bring your attention to the abdominal movements occurring right now.

- But don't think about them; just know them.

- Rising... falling...

- Rising... falling...

- This is our base camp. If you find the mind has wandered just bring it back to the breath event/moment.

- Rising... falling...

- Rising... falling...

- Rising... falling...

- Rising... falling...

To come out of the meditation

- Gently flex your fingers and toes

- Slowly open your eyes. Allow the light to come in

- Avoid looking at anything or anyone in particular

- Now stretch if you need to

- Come back into the space

Well done. Now practice this regularly.

4. Seeing

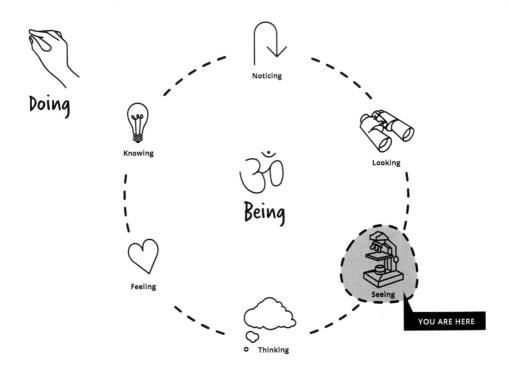

Doing

Noticing

Knowing

Looking

Being

Feeling

Seeing

YOU ARE HERE

Thinking

Fig 20. Seeing. Where you can discover how to open up to your awareness.

We are now going to move on a little further and expand our practice.

We have arrived at Seeing, where we are going to develop our meditation skills and with practice begin to deepen our perception and ability to be still, focused and observe in a particular way. Please remember though this is not a stage; it's simply a different aspect of the same thing.

Having previously explored how to direct attention, this space is about learning to manage, maintain and shape attention towards a deeper experience. This practice corresponds with the yogic practice of Dharana (concentration meditation), where we learn to link awareness to a particular meditation object, in this case sensations in the body and sound, until the field of awareness becomes singular, focused and one with moment-by-moment experience.

We are going to explore a part of yoga science called samapatti (absorption).

"As a flawless crystal absorbs what is placed before it, so the settled mind is transparent to whatever it meets - the seer, the process of seeing or the objects seen. This is samāpatti - the state of mental absorption" [8]

At first reading this may seem a little opaque, maybe even after the tenth reading it still doesn't make any sense. But be patient because this is one of those moments when the true meaning comes not through analysis or intellectual reasoning, but a flash of insight manifested through meditation practice. The mind becomes like a mirror reflecting back to you what is really happening with no judgements, no interpretations, no interference — just you, your insight and the world as they really are.

I describe meditation as **'being aware of being aware, or paying attention to paying attention'.** So when we learn to 'see' more, we develop a more harmonious, creative and open response to the moment. We open up to a new and wider perspective.

---

8 *Effortless Being: The Yoga Sutras of Patanjali. Translated by Alistair Shearer*

In the previous section, 'Looking', we were watching the breath as it came and went without any interference or desire to change the process. We also noted that as we did this, we began to build a deeper shift of awareness which links with the core concept that it's the body that is breathing — not you. All we needed to do was watch. We are now going to introduce **two more meditation objects from the Doing field:**

1. **Physical sensations** that occur within the body, that result from simply being still and sitting.

2. **Sound** that occurs either in the body or most likely around you.

Notice again that both these experiences come to you. Sensation arises in the body, while sound travels towards you mostly from the outside.

Meditation Object — Sensation

When we have been sitting for a while, the body begins to feel restless, with areas of pressure and sensation that arise in the body having been still for a certain amount of time. Of course, you can move if you want to, to relieve any pressure but ideally we want to keep the body in its position and use the experience we are feeling as a meditation object. Similarly, there may be areas of tension or stress in the body that have been with you for a while. As I said, all experience is useful regardless of how you feel or think about it. This is key to this next practice.

As with the breathing meditation object, we want to allow body sensation to also enter into our field of awareness. Unlike breathing however, which is constant, sensations will come and go, have different intensity and appear in a multitude of different locations, sometimes unexpectedly. And that's the whole point:

we want to be with things just as they are, as they arise, and not be surprised or want to shift, respond or shape them in any way.

Adding sensation as a meditation object

All sensation is happening within the body through the nervous system and felt in the mind. Similarly, the body, the sensation and then the feeling of the sensation is manifesting inside the Doing field. The sensation is ultimately not you.

We start by coming back into our core meditation position. We then get started by carrying out our Noticing technique, running through the body and then into our breathing object. You might stay with the breathing object for a while until a physical sensation begins to emerge through your awareness.

Don't go searching for physical sensation. Let it come to you and it will just be. Be open to it. A typical sensation might be pressure in the buttocks, around your lower back, perhaps in the shoulders or in the back of the neck. These are sensations that arise simply as a result of sitting upright in alertness.

There may be other sensations too, such as areas of tension; maybe you're feeling tired or there's a pain in the body caused by an injury or just bad posture. Again don't push these away, they are all useful experiences. Similarly, there will be gentler, softer and perhaps more distant sensations occurring in the body purely as a result of adopting your sitting posture. You may feel the hands gently resting together, particularly the thumbs if you are using the mudra hand position. You may feel the arms resting, falling and relaxing downwards across the front of the body into your lap, gently pulling your shoulders down. You may feel the sensation of lifting the upper body through the crown of the head to keep you alert, or maybe the buttocks or lower back in the angle of the chair.

In reality, the body is sensing all of the time, and most of those points of contact go largely unnoticed. Now we are going to notice them, pay attention to them but without judgement or interference.

So whatever sensations you're aware of as they come to you, don't worry about trying to know all of them together, or worrying about which sensation to choose, just go with the one that is the most intense and most obvious at that moment. It will change as you progress — the key thing is to just know and let go moment-by-moment.

Whatever sensation you choose to observe, just note and label the experience **sensation, sensation, sensation**. You might need to only label it once but if it persists, repeat your meditation object labelling, sensation. In labelling we are noting what is happening as it arises and then by not interfering with it, we are letting it go.

For many, using sensation as meditation objects can be the primary practice. But to begin with, just notice what happens to the sensation as you observe.

You may notice that the physical sensation of feeling, created by whatever is happening in the body, will eventually fall away. This is interesting. Once we begin to know how to simply watch, rather than react to what is happening, the whole character of the event will change.

The softening or retreating of sensation signifies a number of core aspects now beginning to emerge in your practice. First of all of course, all pain is transmitted in the brain. The body has pain receptors but the actual characterisation of the pain is felt in the brain. So once the mind becomes still and settled through the deliberate practice of non-attachment, the pain becomes less intrusive.

In reality, what is happening is the pain is still there, it's just that we have changed our relationship to it. This is a major learning event in that we do not have to be a victim to how we feel. We can be free. It also tells us that everything that happens in the Doing field comes and goes, it passes, nothing is permanent, which means it's not real.

This is why meditation is so useful for people coping with day-to-day pain and particularly those who are struggling with Post-Traumatic Stress Disorder and other trauma.

Practice: Meditation using sensation

- Again, settle into your formal meditation position and come into your alert and relaxed posture. Place the backs of your hands on your upper thighs or rest them in your lap and explore the more traditional hand position of cosmic mudra described earlier. Let the arms relax, feet flat on the floor if you are sitting in a chair and drop the chin gently, while softly closing the eyes and breathing through the nose.

- Start by checking into the body, utilising your noticing technique, beginning with the fingers and toes. Observe the body for a moment without any judgement or preconception. Remember the body is sitting for you. Just be with the body as it is and remind yourself that everything flows.

- Now we begin to draw our attention towards the body breathing. Remember this is our foundation base camp practice, be still and observe the body breathing. Continue to watch as you use your labelling technique – rising... falling and so on. The intention is to expand and build that bubble of awareness around and through you.

- As you begin to nurture this deep space of awareness we allow another object to flow into our awareness space. This time physical sensations in the body. It doesn't matter what type of sensation you are experiencing, it could be just as a result of sitting in the chair or on the floor or maybe there's another sensation – some tension or injury. Whatever sensation is dominant, let it flow into your awareness space and observe without attachment.

- Use your labelling technique: as a particular sensation passes through simply label the event sensation.....sensation....

- Try not to define or identify sensation as a particular thing or experience. Avoid judgements of 'that's uncomfortable', 'that hurts', 'I need to move'.... just watch, observe without attachment...sensation...sensation

- After a few moments you'll notice the sensation you're observing will gently pass and fall away. It appears to empty and soften. Remember: it's not you having the sensation, it's the body. You are simply observing, acting as a witness.

- Other sensations may arise. Treat them the same way. Just observe them without attachment and without interference. If after a while there are no particular sensations arising into your awareness, return back to observing the breath. The body breathing.

- Remember, body sensations are happening in the Doing field. They will flow, rise and fall. There may be more than sensation that arises. Sit with this ever-changing flow for a while until it's time to stop.

As before, when you are ready, gently lift out of your meditation

- Flex your fingers and toes

- Slowly open your eyes. Allow the light to come in

- Avoid looking at anything or anyone in particular

- Now stretch if you need to

- Come back into the space

Adding hearing as a meditation object

We can use sound in exactly the same way body sensation is used. However, with sound, our observation of a meditation object changes. We do not need to reach out for sound but instead sound approaches us. The ear is always in receiving mode. Learning to hear as an object of meditation emphasises how in modern meditation we act as a witness, simply receiving the experience of things just as they are, as they happen. Sound does not change because we choose to listen to it, it just is. However, when we get this aspect of sound as a meditation object and let it come without interference, judgement or analysis, it internalises our experience and helps to create and know a sense of that inner space.

This aspect of meditation may already be familiar to you. Anyone who has laid half awake late at night and followed the sound of, say, a distant motorbike passing by will have experienced that

deep and satisfying sense of place and moment as the sound
passes and expands through your awareness.

The sound is just the sound. You may have had a similar
experience on a summer afternoon, through the warm silence
the droning of a small light aircraft somewhere in the distance
again emphasises that deep and sudden sense of being alive
in a particular place just for a moment or two. If you have had
these experiences then you will recognise this aspect of modern
meditation using sound as an object. Remember sound emerges,
exists and is perceived as an object within your Doing field.
Similarly, the hearing of the sound is also happening within
your nervous system and your body, which is also in your
Doing field.

Many different sounds may come towards you while in
meditation. Sound outside in the street, sound elsewhere in
the building you're in, maybe even sound in the room you're
in. Any sound can be used as a meditation object — even the
background drone of the air conditioning in the office can be an
effective meditation sound object.

Sharp, intrusive noises, such as people talking and the radio
or television are not so useful. As I have mentioned, the mind
automatically will want to direct itself towards human speech
and try to understand what is being said. Sharp noises will
break your flow and concentration. We are going to be open to
sound, we welcome it but would not reach out to grab it — it
should come to you.

When sound does come we simply observe and develop our
sense of non-attached witnessing by utilising our labelling
technique. As we watch sound flow through our awareness, we

simply label the process hearing... hearing... hearing, so that we can build our non-reactive, non-attached open awareness to what is happening in that moment.

Practice: Hearing Meditation

We start by coming back into our original meditation position. Begin by going through the Noticing body scan sequence as described earlier, starting with fingers and toes and gradually building your sense of the body in its position.

Then when you are feeling settled into the body begin observing your first meditation object, the breath with your rising and falling noting technique, keep this going until at some point in your meditation an additional meditation object of sound will rise up into your awareness space. It might be the sound of a passing car or aeroplane, maybe the wind in the trees outside or a ticking clock. Whatever it is, allow the sound to come to you as it is without you interfering, judging or describing what the sound is. Don't stray into thoughts such as 'that's my neighbour's car I can hear, I wonder where they're going?' This aspect of judging and interfering with what is happening as it's happening will take you out of the present moment. Instead, we are just labelling the experience of sound and using the mental label 'hearing'. You can either use the label once, or repeat as the sound moves through your awareness.

After a while, the sound will pass and you can return back to your rising and falling breathing meditation. Try to maintain your open non-judgemental seeing throughout all of this. There is no 'you' or 'I' in the whole process. Just hearing and the sense of presence and oneness that emerges.

Well done. Now practice this regularly too and add it to your Noticing and Looking exercises when you feel you are comfortable with it.

5. Thinking

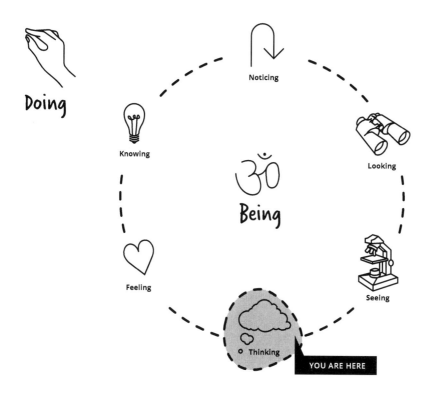

Doing

Knowing

Noticing

Being

Looking

Feeling

Seeing

Thinking

YOU ARE HERE

Fig 21. Thinking. Where you can discover how to tackle the voice in your head.

This part helps us move towards the heart of meditation practice.

It's important to remind ourselves about one of the meditation misconceptions here. Meditation is **NOT** about a psychological suppression or repression of thoughts and emotions. **In meditation we are NOT trying to stop, suppress or block off thinking, feelings and emotions,** but simply make a cognitive shift towards a different sort of relationship.

With meditation, we learn to change how we perceive and interact with thoughts. As we observe and become more aware of our body, breath, senses and surroundings, we also begin to be more aware of our thinking process.

This shift towards observing our thoughts, rather than being our thoughts is a huge moment in one's meditation journey. Remember when we are in meditation we are not ignoring what is happening. We don't close off; we open up. We don't switch off; we switch on.

We are learning to consciously see our own thoughts as they arise. Consciously witnessing and observing thinking is part of our shifting process. It sets us free and allows us to see things as they really are, as they rise, flow and fall moment-by-moment.

We begin to notice, look and then see patterns of thoughts and emotions that are flowing constantly.

We talked earlier about everything being in flow, and that includes your thoughts and your thinking process. As humans though, our problem is that mental flow is far from being in our control. It is very often in a state of agitation and flux. It's no coincidence that the Sanskrit word for mental fluctuation and agitation described in the yoga sutras is **vritti**, meaning whirlpool.

How many times have you felt that your thinking seems to just go round and round, gradually pulling you down until it's overwhelming and drowning you? A whirlpool in your head that draws you ever downwards is a powerful metaphor. So when we meditate we can begin to reduce the intensity of those whirlpools, or learn to swim more effectively in order to keep out of them.

Letting thoughts go

If you are not your thoughts, you can objectify them, you can make them into a meditation object and like all the other objects you've been exploring, they simply pass you by. This concept can get a mixed reaction. Some might be relieved that they are not their thoughts after all and enjoy a sense of release and freedom that comes with this sudden realisation.

Others assume thinking, and particularly the thinking happening exclusively inside their head, is everything. Surely without thoughts you are nothing, you don't exist? In fact the opposite is true.

In other words, you exist first as a conscious individual, as 'I am' (your Being field), before your thoughts start to get in the way and tell you something else (your Doing field). If we go with Descartes' model, that we referred to earlier, we are effectively projecting what we think is happening over what is actually happening. This will always lead to confusion and unhappiness. And it's a state of mind that many of us living in the fast-paced modern world are very familiar with.

Meditation is not what you think! In other words, if you manage to settle your thinking processes and change your relationship to them, you don't suddenly cease to exist. It's actually the opposite. Think about being in a deep, dreamless sleep. Here your brain produces delta waves, which are associated with the deepest levels of relaxation, a stronger immune system and restorative healing. In a sense you have stopped thinking, or at least you have stopped responding to your thinking because you are not conscious of it. For a short while you are not your thoughts, and yet you are still here. The result is rejuvenating. So our lives are not solely reliant on our thinking; in fact, when we manage to change our relationship to them, in this case unconsciously during deep sleep, things change for the better.

So when we learn to let thoughts pass by, we are consciously recalibrating our response and relationship, which will then ultimately change how we see the world that surrounds us, and most importantly how we feel about ourselves.

We let them go and we feel better for it. This takes practice and modern meditation is the key.

So how do I do it?

It's simple. All you need to do is see your thoughts in a different way. For example your thoughts are just a collection of ideas, assumptions and experiences that you have gathered together into a bundle of habits and beliefs over time. You weren't born with the thoughts that you have right now and it's very likely that the thoughts you own right now won't be yours in the future. Thoughts come and go, as they are a process; in many ways thoughts think themselves. In the worst case, thoughts just go round and round and form a habit, meaning you often can't let them go.

To know that ultimately 'you are not your thoughts or your feelings' comes as a great relief to some people, knowing that with practice they can choose to be free from painful, often debilitating, thinking. One way of learning to let thoughts go by is to observe them.

This is the secret of modern meditation. Seeing thoughts as objects, simply coming and going, requires a simple change in perspective, a small cognitive shift which is at the heart of **beanddo** modern meditation.

Even though you can't see your thoughts you certainly primarily experience them, in the way they make you feel, but also in how you respond to your experience and then react accordingly.

It's important to know that almost every thought you have comes in one of two types:

1. Thoughts about the future — thoughts about what might happen or you want to happen.

2. Thoughts about the past — thoughts about things that have happened and you want to rewrite.

This often comes as a surprise to many people because most of us are hardly able to take a step back and watch a thinking process. We spend a great deal of time suffering, worrying about what has happened or what might happen and then how you adapt and change things in response to a basically fictional and misleading account of what is happening. To coin a contemporary phrase, most of the time your thinking is a purveyor of 'fake news', or 'alternative facts'. And because each thought is either trying to rewrite what has happened, or planning to second guess what might happen, you are hardly ever in the present. You are distracted and drawn into that whirlpool of confusion, illusion and misunderstanding.

Of course we can have thoughts about the past and the future which are comforting, uplifting and hopeful. Sometimes it's nice to think back on pleasant events, or make plans with excitement about what might happen. Although we like these thoughts and they are pleasant, this again may well turn out to be untrue.

Next time you find yourself running over a particular train of thought, ruminating over a particular thought process that's repeating itself ad nauseam, just take a step back for a moment and watch the thought. This process does get easier with regular meditation practice.

We spend a great deal of time and mental energy trying to second guess and imagine the best possible outcome for future circumstances. It's exhausting and in the end pointless, because none of the circumstances that you are describing to yourself are real. And that's the crux of it. When we learn the tools of being totally present with meditation, your thoughts naturally begin to settle. Thoughts cannot exist in the here and now, so it therefore leaves the mind clear, open and receptive.

This revelation comes from knowing that thoughts are not facts, they are not real and they are not you. You may have thoughts, but they don't belong to you. Thoughts manufacture each other, until they create one long train of thought. We seem to have little control over this. However, learn to step back, observe and know that this is the beginning of learning and knowing how to change it.

Living inside your own snow globe

We spend a great deal of our time inhabiting an enclosed world of our own design.

When we choose to be distracted by thinking, instead of responding to how others and the world really are, we find ourselves living inside a self-constructed mental world, which is basically an illusion covering over what is really happening. This has a huge impact on how we operate in the world, how we see the world and how we feel about the world. It's like living inside your head, as opposed to living on Earth.

You can imagine this enclosed world as being inside your own snow globe. You very rarely see the world beyond because it is mostly obscured by snowflakes, which swirl and distract every time the snow globe is shaken and agitated. I often use this device in class. When the snow globe is still and held firmly in one place, the snowflakes begin to settle, allowing a clear view in and out of the snow globe. It is only then that the contents of the snow globe reveal themselves.

There are only two aspects of you that are always in the present. Your body and your breath. To put it more accurately, you inhabit a body that breathes for you. The body is always present, unlike your mind, where your thinking spends most of its time either in the past or in the future. This is why we start meditation with the body and breath, because they are the anchor points that keep us connected to the moment.

Let's return to the body again and the horizontal/vertical diagram we described earlier in the book. If the body is always present in the moment then it's located where the horizontal outer experience and the more inner vertical experience intersect. When we apply this to our mental thinking space, the horizontal line connects past and future, while the vertical line connects the here and now.

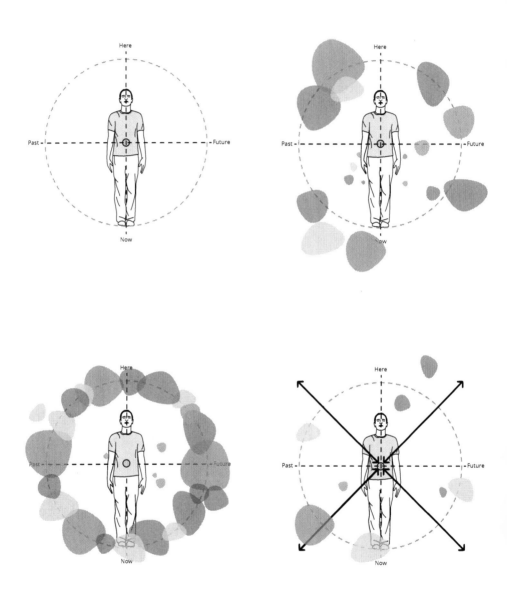

Fig 22. Tackling living in our own mental snow globe

PART TWO

1. Think of horizontal and vertical axes as a clock face with the horizontal connecting past and future and the vertical connection here and now. They intersect where your body is located in the present.

2. Notice how thoughts arrive in two variations. Thoughts about what has happened and what might happen. Because of this they can't exist in the present.

3. If our attention is constantly caught up in this thinking cycle through attempting to manage, interfere and change different thoughts they get more powerful, eventually linking together to create an enclosing mental bubble or snow globe. The result is that we can only see the world through a veil of our own thoughts and self-created constructs (This is known as Maya, in Sanskrit, which translates as self created illusion).

4. But when we meditate regularly we learn to be still to direct our attention towards simply watching the process of thinking, thoughts will eventually decouple and settle. The results will be frequent moments of clarity as you begin to connect outwards to the world, others and yourself with more certainty.

So this self created illusion is defined more commonly as a comfort zone, a place which you are used to and work very hard to stay inside of. But a meditation practice, with its emphasis on finding the centre of the moment, begins to challenge this situation. It's a matter of where we place our attention.

If we keep it fixed towards the enclosing cocoon of thoughts, then we continue to be distracted, feeding the process of thinking, which only gets thicker and more opaque. If however, through meditation practice, we learn the skills for directing attention inward towards the moment, we begin to cultivate that held stillness. We stop shaking and agitating the snow globe and thoughts as snowflakes begin to settle, and an inner clarity and stillness is revealed.

First of all, we may notice that some of the thinking that dominates us begins to lose its colour and little by little becomes less opaque. We may also notice that particularly negative streams of thinking begin to fall away and our world opens up. We begin to see things more clearly, seeing reality as it really is rather than what we think it is. This feels liberating and cleansing. What is really happening is the thinking process has not stopped, it's just that we have changed our relationship to it. We have modified and shifted our viewpoint.

Once our thoughts don't have our attention, we begin to watch and witness them, rather than be them. We begin to know how to not identify or own them, enabling us to let go.

But the mind is still there

It's important to know that the mind is not reduced or switched off in this state. Only the obscuring thoughts that flow across and through the mind are impacted. The mind becomes and stays lucid, clear and sharp as its real power to know, be aware and realise becomes clear.

In a sense, as thoughts begin to settle, the true nature of the mind is exposed, which is like a mirror reflecting back to you a truer and deeper reflection of what is really going on. Once we realise this, we can use this natural shifting as a vital resource time and time again.

This helps to build resilience and reduce resistance and stress because we increase our perspective. We see things as they really are... not what we think they are.

This is the secret to modern meditation. It takes practice, but after a while we can be in a different place. The world changes from a place where we might think we know what is going on, to really knowing what is going on. When our world changes from thinking to knowing, the possibilities are endless.

Introducing the thinking object into your practice

This is perhaps the most challenging technique to weave into our new world experience. Thinking, like breathing, sensing and hearing are meditation objects within our Doing field. If that's the case then it means that Thinking, the process of thinking or even individual thoughts, like your body and your breathing, is not you. We can watch our thoughts in the same way we learnt to watch sensations, sound and breathing as they fluctuate and flow within our awareness.

We learn to let the thoughts 'flow without interruption'.

Witnessing the flow of mind: Witnessing our thoughts is an important aspect of meditation practice. Witnessing the thought process means having the ability to observe the natural flow of the mind, while not being disturbed or distracted. This brings a peaceful state of mind, which allows the deeper aspects of meditation to unfold.

However, usually what happens is that **we don't even notice single thoughts come up.** They connect to create a long train of thought that transports us away from where we are and what we are doing. Luckily, thoughts do tend to come as singular, even if they do not 'feel' like that, as they link and combine together into this train.

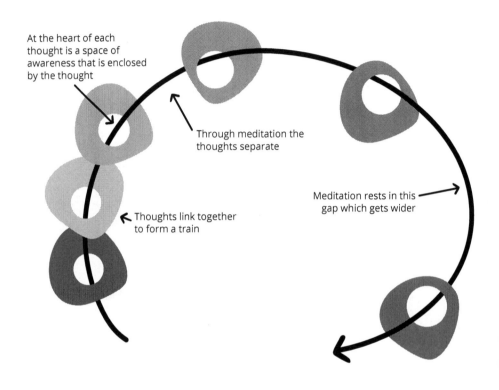

At the heart of each thought is a space of awareness that is enclosed by the thought

Through meditation the thoughts separate

Meditation rests in this gap which gets wider

Thoughts link together to form a train

Fig 23. Observing the gaps between thoughts

As we develop our witnessing, we catch the thought, spot it or detect it as it arises into our conscious awareness. It does not matter what the thought or object is, just allow the image to emerge on its own. It also does not matter whether you literally 'see' with your inner eye or not. Whether you 'see' or do not 'see' with your inner eye, you still are well aware of what images or impressions are arising.

We then witness by labelling the object or experience as thinking, thinking, thinking.

It is natural for thought patterns to do two things:

1. It is natural for thoughts to arise.

2. It is natural for thoughts to gently fall back to the place from which they came.

When that happens we notice there is a space which begins to open between, behind, around or in the centre of each thought. The train of thought gets decoupled. The film playing in your head slows down or appears less distracting.

Letting go is a core meditation skill that can be used in any situation we find ourselves in. Learning to literally let go of a thought is far better than some techniques of getting rid of, or closing off, thoughts and emotions.

This is the art of letting go. It is an ability that few of us have ever been trained to do, but one that we can train ourselves in.

As this skill - of learning to witness and let go of thought patterns is developed - it becomes clearer how this complements the practice of concentrating the mind. Instead of the concentration being a means of suppressing thoughts and emotions, thereby preventing meditation, the field of consciousness is actually expanded from a witnessing stance and deeper meditation is experienced.

Practice: Meditation using thoughts

- Settle into your formal meditation position and come into your alert and relaxed posture.

- Start by checking into the body, utilising your Noticing technique, beginning with the fingers and toes. Observe the body for a moment without any judgement or preconception. Just be with the body and remind yourself that everything flows.

- You may move on towards your breathing meditation in order to settle in and help you focus and become present in your awareness.

- Other objects may also begin to flow into your awareness space such as sensation or sound. Again, you can observe these without attachment as you have done before and just be with them as they rise and fall.

- Remember: you are not your body or your mind. Your body is breathing for you, your mind is thinking for you. So, just as with sensation, breathing and hearing, we simply allow thoughts to appear.

- Just allow each thought whatever it might be to arise on its own. Don't connect with each thought, don't identify or fuse with the feeling, expectation or thought. Just watch them. Witness them by labelling the thought object or experience as 'thinking'. Don't attach yourself to the thoughts, simply label them and let them go.

- You may need to label more than once as a thought passes. Thinking... thinking... thinking.

- After a while, like all other meditation objects, particular thoughts or even the whole thinking process begins to settle. The colour, the content and the feeling infused with each begins to mellow and soften.

- Keep the practice going, noticing when you perhaps connect to a passing thought and travel along with it. Don't worry if this happens, as it will happen often. The key is to notice you have got on board with a particular thought and have allowed it to take you away from the present moment.

- If you find yourself in a space with no particular thoughts arising, be present and rest in the stillness and sense of unbounded openness and freedom that this moment suddenly reveals. That space of stillness and freedom in between and underneath your thinking mind.

As before, when you are ready, gently lift out of your meditation

- Flex your fingers and toes

- Slowly open your eyes. Allow the light to come in

- Avoid looking at anything or anyone in particular

- Now stretch if you need to

- Come back into the space

The more you can become a witness to your thoughts, the less control those thoughts have over you, increasing your freedom of choice, what you can do and how you see the world. **Witnessing** prepares you for making everything you do anytime, anywhere, a meditation.

Of course, all thoughts appear real because they prompt us to respond with either an action, another thought or a feeling in the mind-body. It's the feeling that tends to stay with us longer.

So we try and stay in that moment before thought becomes an action, before thought becomes a word, before thought becomes a feeling — even before a thought becomes a thought. The more we do this, the more the moment around that space expands. It provides you with an opportunity to reflect and respond rather than react. Even when you appear to be acting spontaneously, you are working from that space of Knowing.

In the next section, we will be looking at the inner consequences of our thinking process and how we can go deeper and further into being free from how we think and how we feel.

6. Feeling

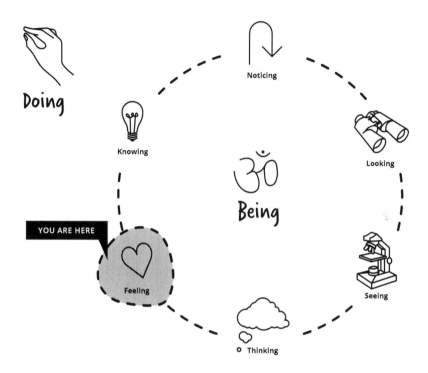

Fig 24. Feeling. Where we learn to be liberated from our thoughts and how they make us feel.

We described earlier that our default position is happiness. We are hardwired to be happy and because of that, **we all want to feel happy.**

Most of us want to avoid being unhappy, so why is it we can't just think happy thoughts and feel positive all of the time, so that we never have to deal with feeling down? Well, firstly that would be boring. Think of all the great art that wouldn't exist without that very human capacity for melancholia. And secondly, meditation teaches us to be with things as they are no matter what they are. As the great poet William Blake in his poem 'Auguries of Innocence' told us, once we know and accept that we are designed to feel both happiness and sadness, we discover a better way through the world.

However, we tend to want to categorise, define, judge and then resolve every experience. We want to feel good about them. When that happens we also take ownership of our own judgement of that experience. We say, 'that is good, this is bad', or 'I don't like this person, I like that person'. All of these thoughts, opinions and assumptions are objects of experience that rise up and flow through the Doing field and are felt in the body. We create all sorts of attachments, from pride and desire, to anger and fear. This reinforces our sense of separateness, isolation and sense of ego. Similarly, the world of work can be full of confrontation, deadlines and challenging people. The world is full of stuff going on. It's in constant flux and it's designed to be that way. The ancient yoga texts tell us if there were not challenges and obstacles in the world there would be no need for yoga and meditation.

"The purpose of the world is to provide us with experience and lead us to liberation"[9]

The world as it is right now, made up of moment-by-moment experiences, no matter how trivial or important, is so that we can practice meditation. It's our relationship to all of those experiences that is the key.

---

9   *Effortless Being: The Yoga Sutras of Patanjali. Translated by Alistair Shearer*

"Man is not troubled by things, but his opinion of them"[10]

So, like everything else, it is our attachment to our feelings that causes pain. Of course we still have feelings - we don't want to deny how we feel - but we can change the way we respond to those experiences.

It might sound counterintuitive but like working with the physical sensation earlier, we don't push those emotionally-stressful experiences away: use them and embrace them. The only way to make progress is when we are open to and accepting of what is.

The previous practice helped us explore how the process of thinking and our attachment to certain thoughts pulls us away from being present. This section is all about how to deal with the mind-body experience of that thinking, ie our feelings and emotions.

We are going to extend and expand our perspective, our practice, from simply witnessing and observing Thinking as a process to how thoughts link to particular feelings or emotions. This is the aspect of meditation practice which helps us build an inner resilience and will — if we let it — set us free and make us stronger.

Yogic science tells us that ultimately we are neither our body or our mind. So by definition we are also not our thoughts or actions — they simply come and go as part of the Doing field

of change. Meditation helps us find a space, a position from

10 *Epictetus*

which to observe the Doing field in action. Then the very act of observation from this position engages and enlivens with the seer, the witness, the observer. The real you as absolute consciousness residing in the Being field.

Becoming free

Our feelings and emotions are linked to how and what we are thinking. We feel emotions 'physically' and 'spatially' in the mind-body field. How we think impacts on the body, all of which happens in the Doing field.

We can get trapped and held captive by the intensity of our feelings and emotions as they grip hold of the body. It can feel like we are being held hostage by them all of the time. They cause disharmony and leave us unbalanced.

We know when we are angry about something, as we feel it in the pit of our stomach and our heart pounds. We want to react in a certain way, change something, or resist to help resolve our pain, as agitating thoughts and feelings impact on how we feel.

Many of us live day-to-day with a gentle, internal sense of apprehension or light dread. We may experience a gentle tightness, which rests in the chest or throat. We constantly feel butterflies, which appear all by themselves, seemingly unrelated to any external events.

Many too will suffer from Sunday night blues. This is a modern condition. The very day you are supposed to be feeling centred, relaxed and calm. The very day that is designed to promote stillness and reflection can also be a day of mounting dread and fear, as thoughts turn to getting back to work in the morning.

For many it can be an acute condition, as those feelings of helplessness and dis-empowerment, linked to anxiety and stress, intensify. And because Sunday night blues is when you iron your clothes, make sure your bag is ready and lunch is made for the next day, each item on your to do list intensifies those feelings.

The feelings associated with the Sunday night blues are all wrapped up with **expectation,** linked to that feeling that maybe you are not doing the right thing or dreading what you imagine is heading your way once you get to work. For some, the Sunday night blues can be tinged with doubt and a little regret. 'Am I doing what I should be doing? Should I be doing something else, be somebody else?' Another week ahead doing the stuff you think you shouldn't be doing. Here is the voice in your head, powering up one's natural negativity bias which eventually overheats.

I know from my own experience that meditation is the key. If you keep focused on that constantly emerging sense of now, you would always be exactly where you were supposed to be, doing exactly what you are supposed to be doing. When you train yourself to be in the present, you can look up out of your mental and emotional agitation and take real notice. Everything will be fine. In fact, everything is fine.

We are all in action. We all have to do something. So why not make what we are doing the whole point? It's all a process, not a destination or a set of fixed points. It's fluid and when we get that moment of being present, it flows.

No more worry. No doubt. No more 'what ifs'… just get on with it.

You will learn that those Sunday night blues were nothing to do with Sunday at all.

You manifest your own feelings of dread if you spend every Sunday attaching labels and concepts to the moment rather than just letting Sunday afternoon be Sunday afternoon. Of course, you can still have those thoughts and concepts. It's okay, but with meditation we uncover a whole new way of just being, no matter what day of the week it is, and no matter how we are feeling, because you know what? Sunday is a concept too; it exists in our head inside the Doing field.

Learn to know that, be free and get to work on Monday morning a whole new person. In fact, the person you are supposed to be, doing the work you are supposed to be doing.

Resistance is futile

A study undertaken at The University of California[11], Berkeley has recently looked at how emotional and mental acceptance, a technique developed through meditation, can bring positive impacts to psychological health. The results show that people who try to resist their negative thoughts and emotions, who try to control and stop them, ended up only intensifying their psychological stress and anxiety.

In contrast, people who learnt to just be alongside their negative thoughts and emotions, rather than push them away, noticed the psychological impact became less intense, eventually falling away. So by embracing what is happening without wanting to

11   *Berkeley News. Feeling bad about feeling bad can make you feel worse. Yasmin Anwar. August 10, 2017*

control it, identify with it or fight it, maximum control is gained.

When we learn to let go through meditation practice we learn to stop resisting. This is often confusing for people who are just starting out.

Surely if you feel bad you should do what you can to make it stop and resist it? Ironically, it is the resisting that intensifies the experience of feeling bad.

The simple change of perspective that meditation nurtures leads to a conscious relationship between inner Being and outer Doing worlds. In short, we are learning to create a space between you and the world. This involves learning to let go, not so that you don't care what really happens, but more so that you are engaged and have a deeper connection to what is happening right here, right now. This is letting go with a purpose.

The middle ground

When we learn to let go and just be alongside experiences, feelings and thoughts, we are occupying 'the middle ground'. In reality, there are no bad or good thoughts or emotions; there are just thoughts and emotions that rise up, stay around for a while and fall away. It's only our judgement and identification with a particular thought or emotion — in other words, your relationship to them — that intensifies the feeling.

"Why, then, 'tis none to you, for there is nothing either good or bad, but thinking makes it so. To me it is a prison. Well, then it isn't one to you, since nothing is really good or bad in itself — it's all what a person thinks about it".[12]

Building resilience

There is often a fusion with the emotions, thoughts and sensations that arise. We need to learn how to break these fusions, to still them, so to allow a deeper underlying response. For example: when we have a feeling, an emotion or pain, we experience it in the body. The sensation arises and then we identify with it, we appropriate it as our ego kicks in and then we say **I am angry, I am unhappy, I am sad, I am fed up**. That fusion between your ego and the object is where suffering begins.

We create our own cycle of emotion. So when we meditate, we are learning to see these moments of fusion and we are learning how to not get caught up in it in a reactive way. Because we experience suffering in only two places – the mind and the body – the purpose of a meditation is to build a space between you and your mind–body. This way we can learn to observe suffering from a distance. We suffer, but our relationship to it changes. The space that we create in meditation helps us build perspective, change our standpoint and reorientate ourselves. If that is the case, we are free from suffering. We nurture our inbuilt resilience and are able to cope with many different types of life circumstances.

This new sense of space and perspective helps build the conditions for resilience. We naturally design ourselves space and time to not be overly swayed or overwhelmed by emotions.

12   *Shakespeare: Hamlet: Act 2, Scene 2*

We begin to manage and fine tune the cycle of impact between what we think and how we feel. This is not to say that we become cold and detached, but more that we deeply feel emotions beyond just what we think about them or how we react against them.

"Meditation has the power to soften sorrow and destroy mental pain. With experience, you develop an intuitive penetrating skill... that makes the knotty issues of life no longer big problems. Life then smoothes out and suffering dissolves."[13]

When we learn to watch and observe feelings as they come and go, good or bad, we notice they begin to loosen their grip on our day-to-day experiences. Our natural inbuilt resilience grows, self-critical judgements fall away and we begin to feel different, positive about what we can do and our potential is no longer caught up in it.

These changes happen automatically. We don't need to probe, analyse or dissect our emotional thinking. That is not helpful and it will build a judgement-fuelled resistance which paradoxically fuses the mind with what it's thinking, which will make it harder. As our ability to examine and observe the thinking process improves and sharpens, we can then start to discriminate more towards what is useful for us.

---

13   *Essential Wisdom of the Bhagavad Gita. Ancient Truths for the Modern World. Jack Hawley*

What's useful and not useful – If you have a negative feeling about yourself or some other person, a feeling that is not useful to your growth, you simply notice it and note that, "This is Not Useful", saying the words internally. Or, you may internally say only the single phrase, "Not Useful". Negativity can continue to control us only when we are not aware of them. When we notice them, and label them as "Not Useful" thoughts, we can deal with those thoughts in positive, useful ways.

When positive, helpful thoughts arise that lead us in the direction of growth and spiritual truths or enlightenment, we can remind ourselves, "This is Useful" or simply, "Useful". Then we can allow those useful thoughts to move into actions.

See your feelings honestly – This is not being negative about yourself, passing judgement on yourself, or calling yourself negative. Rather, it is a process of honestly naming the thought patterns and feelings as they are: a negative experience.

Instead, promote the positive, useful thoughts. Observe without attachment the negative thoughts that are not serving you well. This may sound like hard work, but it really isn't and with practice you will find there is no such thing as positive or negative thoughts.

Non-attachment to feelings

When we apply the **beanddo** meditation algorithm to a particular feeling that we may be experiencing, we can begin to break the cycle of thoughts and feelings. If we are feeling panicked, scared, or fearful, we directly observe those feelings in our body and mind.

Simply acknowledge what is happening through observation

without judgement, without wanting to interfere, shape or push away what is happening. We need to be with them as they are. We let them be. At first this may seem counterintuitive but meditation training shows us how to let go and be in the flow of things. The insight cultivated shows us that it's a much more effective technique than fighting panic. There's a wise saying:

"Whatever you resist, persists."

Introducing Feeling object into your practice

We are now going to add this new meditation object to our practice. We have learnt to direct a sustained, non-judgemental awareness to our breathing to sensations, sound and thinking. Now we move towards feelings.

When we are undertaking our sitting practice, we cultivate an awareness where we experience everything as a passing, flowing phenomena. When you practice, you become a still point of observation around which everything flows. You see that nothing really stays, nothing is particularly important and nothing lasts. That's true of our emotions and feelings, even though at the time of sitting that may not feel true. All of our feelings and emotions occur in the Doing field.

Depending on where we are and how we feel, we may just want to work with one meditation object, as we have said before. So in this case, if you are feeling particularly unhappy or troubled, in an endless cycle of pain in the mind-body, then you can move swiftly in your practice towards using that feeling as a meditation object.

As we are going deeper with our practice, remember to be gentle and make haste slowly. If at any point you feel overwhelmed by what you are feeling, stop. It might be that this particular part of meditation practice is not right for you at the moment. Instead simply use the other objects and change will come.

Remember also our intention here is NOT to follow thoughts and feelings to their root cause. We are not trying to understand them or analyse them. We are learning to be with them, watch them and then let them pass by.

Practice: Feeling Meditation

- Settle into your formal meditation position and come into your alert and relaxed posture. Place your hands into your cosmic mudra position, let the arms relax, feet flat on the floor (shoes off) and drop the chin gently, while softly closing the eyes and breathing through the nose.

- Start by checking into the body, utilising your Noticing technique, beginning with the fingers and toes. Observe the body for a moment, without any judgement or preconception. Just be with the body and remind yourself that everything flows.

- After a moment or two, when you feel the experience of the practice is beginning to blossom, turn your attention towards the abdomen and use your breathing object meditation. Stay here for a while until you notice other meditation objects arising in your awareness space, such as a sound sensation.

- There will be thoughts too. Again, observe them as before and label them. You will need to repeat this shift often.

- Now allow a particular feeling you may be experiencing in

the moment to enter into your awareness space. You will know intuitively what this feels like. It will be a sensation in the mind-body field, but it will feel different from physical sensation, which would tend to come to you from a specific direction. The sensation of feeling will have a more opaque, flowing and somatic nature. It doesn't particularly matter if it's pleasant or unpleasant. But you will recognise it and what it is.

- Without trying to change it or eliminate it in any way, just witness what is happening, as it is happening. Now observe the sensation and label it, 'feeling', 'feeling', 'feeling'.

- Keep going gently, just simply witnessing the experience as it comes and goes. After a while you will begin to notice the 'colour' of the particular feeling begin to softly empty. You may sense that the feeling is still there, and that as we observe and witness, our relationship to it changes, as it remains in the Doing field while we observe from our Being field.

- The mind may wander and you may become distracted. That's normal, just bring your observation back to the sense of feeling and maintain your labelling.

- Your sense of being present to the moment will deepen and with it, an expansion of awareness, insight and stillness.

- Stay with your meditation experience for as long as you planned. You may have been adding other objects as well to maintain the practice.

Then, when ready, gently lift out of your meditation:

- Gently flex your fingers and toes

- Slowly open your eyes. Allow the light to come in

- Avoid looking at anything or anyone in particular

- Now stretch if you need to

- Come back into the space

Going beyond thoughts and feelings

Try and practice this with courage. Don't analyse, judge or compare. There are no good or bad feelings – there is just feeling and it's an integral part of being alive with a mind and body. Knowing that helps you be 'alive' to life. It will be challenging, as most likely you have developed all sorts of tactics, responses and habits to deal with how you feel. But with persistence there will be a change, a shift in how you feel and react. It will be subtle at first. But what had previously been filled with apprehension, for example those Sunday night blues, seem to empty out and soften until you hardly notice that they have disappeared.

So as we continue to move around the map, we are starting to go beyond and behind the entire thought process, to the joy of simply being. It's here we can start asking different sorts of questions, from 'where am I?' to 'who am I?' The answer comes perhaps not in words but in experience, insight and sometimes surprising action as you move away from what you thought you were and what you thought was your comfort zone. This is the beginning of liberation. With practice you will begin to see that who you really are is what is left after letting go of your feelings and thoughts.

This leads us to the next three map locations of Knowing, Being and Doing, where we get closer to knowing, being and doing who you really are.

7. Knowing

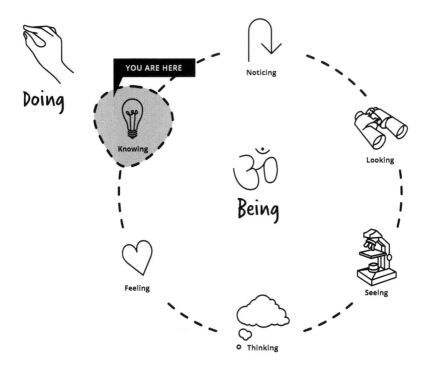

Fig 25. Knowing. Where you can discover how to use your inner compass

Up until now, you may have thought that much of what we've been talking about is to do with concentration, directing attention and sustaining it. And in many cases that's exactly what we've been doing. Now with knowing, we begin to explore the true reality of what meditation is, beyond focused attention, labelling and mental witnessing.

As we continue with the process of meditation, we are beginning to experience that point where Being and Doing connect. We can call this place our centre of consciousness and as we recognise it, we learn to stay there and nurture it. With practice, we begin to notice an expansion that emerges seemingly from the inside out. Concentration contracts and is replaced by an effortless **knowing of a state of consciousness** and awareness. We may have felt we were aware before but now we are moving towards being aware of our awareness. Once this shift is explored our 'insight' grows and we begin to develop a deeper knowing experience that rests under our thoughts, actions and feelings.

"By the clarity of intuitive perception everything can be known."[14]

This new sense of Knowing provides access to a better, more creative, healthier, optimistic and resilient version of yourself. This is the part of you that is real and always available. And it's here where we begin to fine-tune and develop our scope and insight towards empowering yourself to be more and do more.

As we progress with our meditation practice, we begin to know that it's less about effort, targets, schemes, strategies and expectations and more about letting go and learning to trust. This comes about with less thinking about what is happening and more about knowing how it is happening and then knowing why.

This cultivation of Knowing is outside of thinking. You might say that knowing is another word for intuition, wisdom, insight and creativity. To know in this sense is to feel and embody what is right for you, what needs doing and which direction you need to go. It is sometimes referred to as **your inner compass**.

When we cultivate Knowing through meditation practice, we are reaping the benefits of the Being field. That part of you knows

---

14   *Effortless Being: The Yoga Sutras of Patanjali. Translated by Alistair Shearer*

who you are and what you need to do. It is that part of you that is never angry, does not need anything and is always joyful. So don't try and think that you know — you just know.

It happens all by itself. This is important. After a while we begin to develop insight into knowing who we are, what we are capable of and what it is we need to do. This new experience is simply an uncovering of what is already there. And it probably won't come as a flashing insight or epiphany (although sometimes it does), but more a gradual unfolding, knowing that provides access to a deeper, innate, more powerful creative source.

Knowing comes with an inbuilt momentum. And things begin to change.

Can you recall those times when you are working on something and you seem to know just what to do? Every action seems to be supported by the previous action and creates the conditions for the next one. Whatever it was you were doing seemed to come effortlessly. Solutions or supportive events or people just seemed to flow towards you. This is the result of knowing our inner teacher, or better still, allowing your inner teacher - your Being field, to flow through into the world of your Doing.

Can you also recall a time when you were wrestling with a certain problem in life? Perhaps an issue at work, a misunderstanding between friends or a problem at home. Here you told yourself 'if only I could find a bit of space' or 'get some perspective', so that you can work things out and know which way to go and what to do. Well that's the space we're heading towards. It's a space where we just seem to know what to do. It is knowing and it's constantly available.

Remember: when you practice meditation, you are preparing the ground for change – like a gardener or farmer preparing the soil or land. We don't force or manipulate, we set the conditions and allow things to happen by themselves, not unlike allowing plants to grow in our garden once we have created the right conditions for them to thrive and blossom. Everything flows, but if we hold on and expect things to be different, we create resistance to the flow, which in turn causes friction.

We know that friction causes a great deal of heat and energy. This is useful when we want to apply the brakes on a car, or generate electricity. However, when it comes to life we often apply resistance. It comes in the form of attachment or avoidance, desire, anger, frustration and greed. When we resist, we are inflexible, we try and hold on to a position or an assumption, which we have always assumed is correct or adopted because it feels safe and comforting. Resistance here generates negative energy which means living in fear — trust your inner compass and allow it to guide you.

This is what is meant by Knowing and meditation reveals this deeper insight. When we get this, we notice a softening of personal attachment to self-created ideas regarding the illusion of I, me and mine. A natural openness and generosity begins to develop. We are living as a real yogi with non-attachment.

When we begin to feel that previous ideas such as 'I am my job, I am my status', 'my reputation, my past, my wants, my desires, my possessions and my beliefs' are limiting, they are shown to be illusions and the source of much unhappiness and discontent. They are nothing more than false identities, illusions that veil over the world as it really is. This is why a certain type of attachment to social media can be so overwhelming and the cause of much unhappiness.

After a while, you may begin to notice your position and perspective on certain life events begins to change. You are already that which you seek. You have everything you need to be a conscious, happy and creative individual. You don't need anything else. Just being present doing what you are doing is enough. It's a process. It's not a place we need to get to or adapt to. Judgement and expectation begin to fall away and you start to see life no longer swinging between opposites and demands, but of an ongoing process of change with you right in the heart of it all.

You're cultivating an ability to accept and respond creatively, effortlessly and productively to every moment-to-moment experience. Similarly, your reactive and defensive negative mindsets and attitudes fall away.

7 ways of Knowing

Cultivating Knowing manifests from where we learn to place our attention. If our attention is primarily captured in the Doing field, then we hardly notice the Being field and the benefits it can bring. But remember: while they represent our outer and inner life, they need to merge together. We enter the Being field through the Doing field and with practice we can learn to make them work together, whenever we need to.

1. **Knowing versus analysing**
   Imagine if you could just know what to do at any given time. It's fine to analyse and weigh up the options, that's a critical skill for most of us, but there will be times when you simply know what to do and trust that intuition. This is more than just gut instinct that comes from experience, this knowing comes from a deeper place.

2. **Accepting versus expecting**
Knowing to let things be just as they are is another benefit for cultivating your deeper sense through meditation. Most of the time, many of us live in a mindset of expectation, of wanting to change things so that they match the world we create in our head. Imagine if we could just see things as they are, and see them for the first time. You'll be amazed to know that everything you need is right there in front of you. You will find you don't need to expect anything to change a great deal. When you accept that you will find the world changes accordingly.

3. **Awake versus asleep**
Knowing means you are wide awake. Being asleep in this context means not taking notice, not paying attention and being distracted. It means following a course of action which has been given to you by others. Instead, choose to be awake, see the world as it is and then know what action and path to follow. You only take the best and most effective route if your eyes are open.

4. **Now versus when**
Life flows in the now. It's only right here in this moment you can effect change, act and create. Everything else is an illusion, so don't wait for conditions to somehow miraculously align themselves for you to be happy, successful and fulfilled. Just know that you are already those things.

5. **Reality versus illusion**
Knowing helps us discriminate between what's real and unreal. Your thoughts and feelings are not real – they are fiction. Knowing this helps you to not be enslaved by your judgements, expectations and assumptions. You are free to

act accordingly. But this deeper sense of knowing means that everything you do is authentic, real and emerging from the real you.

6. **Letting go versus holding on**
   Knowing when to let go is vital. You can't control everything and you shouldn't try to. If you spend all your time holding onto your status, your identity and your ego, it means you missed the point. Holding on is restrictive, limiting and ultimately debilitating. When we cultivate our sense of Knowing, we feel empowered and more confident to be with ourselves just as we are, to just let go and be.

7. **Flowing versus resisting**
   This leads us to knowing that we are a still point gently located in the heart of things as they flow by. Be open to that, don't resist change. Instead guide it and be a conduit for that change. Resistance causes heat, noise, friction and pain.

This new perspective on any given situation allows you to remain directly connected to what is happening, but also as something more. The seven aspects noted above may look like choices in life, but in fact they're not. We don't need to decide between one or the other. When we let go and simply observe what's happening in the Doing field, we automatically cultivate the benefits of inhabiting the Being field. This is the Knowing aspect of meditation practice.

You begin to feel yourself as a wide open space of pure awareness, which is different from just thinking about being aware or noticing what is happening around us. This deeper knowing of awareness places us inside our Being field but also as a knowing participant and collaborator with our Doing field. We feel distinct and separate from our desire to judge, want, resist, manipulate and all the other feelings and emotions that arise in the Doing field. This shift tells us we are fine. Right here, right now in this moment everything is okay. We can stop struggling, resisting and causing more and more unwanted friction in our lives.

So what is it exactly that we are knowing? It is a deeper connection to the mind and body — this is an instrument of action and change prompted and inspired by your sense of Being, your centre of consciousness. It's this part of you that knows what to do as it watches and experiences the mind-body in action in the Doing field.

We experience our action in the world through our body flow, but while we are in that flow, our body actions are in fact separate from it. We are connected but there is also a space between ourselves and the mind-body — it's this space which deepens and strengthens through meditation practice. It's where we exist.

To cultivate and utilise our 'knowing' facility, we will start to look at how meditation practice opens up to a deeper, inner wisdom insight — the intuitive faculty which we all share. The Knowing faculty is deeply linked to creativity, which in turn is connected to one's own sense of purpose - **Dharma** - as it is sometimes referred to, meaning one's essential nature, duty or direction in life.

One could say that as one's sense of knowing is enlivened and felt, meditation practice swings from an inner to an outer process of change, growth and intervention. The Knowing point in our practice is where Being and Doing collapse into each other.

It is at this stage that we begin to move inwards, towards our Being field, as it links and shapes our Doing field. We begin to know insight and intuition, and our natural inbuilt wisdom.

When we open up to our insight through meditation practice we gain access to a natural, everlasting inner resource.

When we nurture our Knowing, we open ourselves up to a whole host of abilities we never knew we had. We begin to know not only who we are, where we are, but also what we need to do. This is our inner compass, that inner sense which tells us when we are on track or when we might be heading in the wrong direction. It can be liberating, but also challenging. But don't worry, because the universe is right behind you once you choose to know rather than want!

"We must be willing to get rid of the life we've planned, so as to have the life that is waiting for us. Follow your bliss and the universe will open doors for you where there were only walls."[15]

What's happening when we just Know?

When we nurture our capacity to know, we begin to reorientate ourselves in the world. We realise that the world is not something we need to master, exploit, challenge or manipulate. The world and what you do – if it comes from your authentic self – makes us participants in the process. We are part of the flow of things. As I mentioned in Part One, the wisest thing to do is to concentrate on where you can make a real and direct difference. Knowing this is the real wisdom behind making happy work.

---

15   Joseph Campbell. The Power Of Myth. With Bill Moyers

When your sense of Knowing is nurtured you begin to have access to a deeper reality. A deeper set of rules, instructions and motivations that are subtly wired into your nervous system. Whenever you forget or are forced to separate from this feeling, you're naturally designed to feel that 'something's off' or 'not right'. These are like messengers signalling you to take notice so that you can take the actions that restore your sense of purpose and get you back on track.

With this in mind we are using meditation here as a reset. As a moment of stillness, in which to allow Knowing to arise. Knowing yourself as wholeness enables you to experience your essential nature, your inner field of Being, that's incapable of being stressed, worried or exploited.

Often you will come into your sitting practice with a particular train of thought regarding something that you are doing. It might be something you are planning for or struggling with. Maybe something at work or a project you are developing that has hit an obstacle or impasse, that needs a shift in momentum or direction, requiring a creative insight or leap forward.

The key is of course to let go and simply watch that train of thought. Allow your meditation to take its course without expectation. More times than not you will come out of your meditation practice with a sense of what you need to do. When I meditate, I like to always keep a notebook or sketchbook and pen handy, to quickly record the insights and the potential ideas that emerge during my sitting practice. Ideally, have it right next to you as you practice so that you can capture the insight quickly.

Moving onwards

As you continue with your meditation practice and cultivate your natural inner Knowing, you will begin to see that on the surface so many of your thoughts and emotions are to do with the 'concept of you' that you have created over time. You realise that you have been working really hard to project a particular type of image, in the way you dress, the way you react to certain people or even the way you think. There is a huge degree of pain and tension in this because it's all to do with what you think should be happening. When you uncover that deeper Knowing, you are free. Knowing in this way is not a reduced version of you, it's the real you! Then you know that there is nothing special to be other than be you, nor anything special to do other than do you.

Knowing is your ultimate **inner resource**. Your whole sense of **Being**. To know, in this way, is to know who you really are and maybe even know your purpose. When you learn to cultivate your inner knowing, you will begin to feel a particular momentum flow through you. To what end, it may not be clear from the start but trust the process and you will at some stage embody your core purpose and the direction it is leading you.

Practice: Knowing meditation

· Settle into your prefered meditation position and come into your alert and relaxed posture. Place your hands into your cosmic mudra position, or rest the backs of your hands on your knees. Let the arms relax, feet flat on the floor (shoes off if you are in a chair) and drop the chin gently, while softly closing the eyes and breathing through the nose.

- Start by checking into the body, utilising your noticing technique, beginning with the fingers and toes. Observe the body for a moment, without any judgement or preconception. Just be with the body and remind yourself that everything flows.

- After a moment or two, when you feel the experience of the practice is beginning to blossom, turn your attention towards the abdomen and use your breathing meditation object. Stay here for a while until you notice other meditation objects arising in your awareness space, such as a sound and sensation.

- There will be thoughts and feelings too. Again, observe them as before and label them. You will need to repeat this shift often.

- As your awareness grows it might be now that you can bring your attention towards a deep, underlying feeling of change and momentum. It is there. It might need answering or responding to. Whatever it is, just be with it and know that it will take care of itself. That it will emerge and unfold as it needs to. No need to resist or struggle, decide or plan. Just sit with this feeling of momentum.

- It might be that this feeling is simply that — a feeling arising in the mind and body, maybe from the chest, or lower back. It doesn't really matter where. Just know that it does not need to be managed, changed, actioned or tackled. Just trust and know this feeling and whatever it is asking you to do, know that you are already doing it. Affirm to yourself that whatever purpose is behind this momentum it is true for you right now. It's happening. It is real in every part of your body.

- Stay with this experience of knowing this momentum, this purpose. It might be that there is no clear picture of what this purpose is other than you know it and feel it. Just stay with it, no need to investigate imagine or strategise, just stay with it.

- Keep going gently, just simply witnessing the experience as it comes and goes. The mind may wander and you may become distracted. That's normal, just bring your observation back to knowing that inner sense of purpose.

Then, when ready, gently lift out of your meditation:

- Gently flex your fingers and toes

- Slowly open your eyes. Allow the light to come in

- Avoid looking at anything or anyone in particular

- Now stretch if you need to

- Come back into the space

Now we move to our final two locations on our map.

8. Being

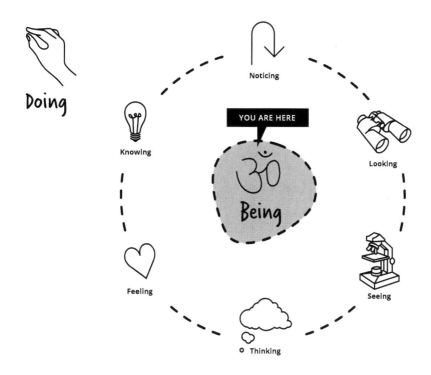

Fig 26. Being. Where you can discover who you really are.

Our meditation practice has allowed us to go diving inwards to the centre, where we arrive and inhabit our Being field and our true feeling of being alive. The innate sense of Being, of oneness and being whole is natural to all of us. However, many of us simply don't take the time to be there.

To mark the location of 'Being' on the map, I have used the Sanskrit yogic symbol, 'AUM' (pronounced OM). This is because there is frankly no other device which encapsulates and conveys 'Being'. AUM takes us back to the earlier part of the book, where I described how meditation works – simply, sustained awareness, moment-by-moment which in turn settles the mind so that it reflects one's essential nature. This is, as the ancient yogis told us, 'unbounded consciousness' from which everything we see, feel, hear and know comes. It's the creative core of you and me, it's nature is joy, which is where I started this book by saying you are already happy, because you too are made of consciousness.

Hearing the message

Meditation opens up the space in which these human qualities already reside. When we learn through meditation to just be and watch with stillness, that sense of Being grows and expands. In this Being space, we are going to touch on the place our meditation practice is naturally taking us. Our felt-sense of Being, which is different and separate from who you think you are in your head, away from any limiting ideas about I, me or mine (your ego). Remember our making happy work algorithm, which is designed to minimise the internal mental noise, so that we can isolate the signal and hear the message, allowing Being and Doing to unify without interference.

The algorithm tells us we are born with happiness already built-in. Wellbeing is hard wired into our systems. **Happiness is the absence of unhappiness,** it's not the other way around. Happiness is our default position.

The more you practice, the more you are aware of what actions, people, distractions and thought processes pull you off-centre and away from your own unique sense of Being. We become sensitive as we begin to go deeper into our meditation practice. Those feelings of 'something not being right' are like messages that are coming from inside us.

They are asking us to realign, to restore or reboot our innate operating system. To get back into just Being.

Who are you?

It should be clear by now that you and I are more than our mind or body. We have thoughts, but they are not us. We don't own thoughts. Thoughts come and go in the Doing field.

But as we have seen, when we start to mistakenly fuse and identify with what we think we are experiencing, we start living in our head, instead of the real world. And if you then start looking for your sense of Being in your head, you will not find it. It's not there. So where then? The answer is that space in the centre of our Being-Doing circle.

I talked earlier about the health warnings in our meditation classes: after practising for a while you may catch yourself smiling at strangers, feeling more positive, healthier, productive and creative. You may have increased energy and are moving more freely in the body. One of the most important health warnings we give is a sudden and unexpected feeling of joy for no apparent reason. A joy that just comes without any connection to where you are, what you're doing or what's happening. Just joy as it is, which is the joy of simply **Being.**

While this is often amusing in class, there is a serious point. We are living in challenging times. We are distracted more than ever from experiencing the joy of simply Being. Ironically, mainstream media and advertising are constantly trying to find new ways of conveying what it's like to live a fulfilled life. For example, buy this car, eat this food, drink that sugary drink or look, dress and sound like this particular celebrity. We are lost to our real selves. The degree of distraction now is at epidemic levels. Particularly now, as your attention has become monetised by internet giants. We know it's particularly problematic for young people, because learning how to **be** is becoming increasingly hard to do. Almost all social media is built around expectation and judgement, which are two of the biggest obstacles to simply just Being. We are invited to like, share and comment continuously. The young are never told the one true fundamental objective of all of us is to know the experience of Being. It's our only responsibility. It's the only thing about ourselves that we need to like and share.

Try these short observation exercises, then ask yourself. Who or what is looking?

Hand gazing

Lift your hand upwards and spread the fingers outwards so that you can look down at the palm of your hand. Maintain your gaze towards the hand as intensely as you can without interruption. Don't concentrate on any one particular area just look at the hand as it is without attachment.

Maintain your gaze. You may want to label the moment and treat the whole thing as an object for meditation so mentally just acknowledge, 'Looking'. You are simply looking at the hand as an object. After a while a degree of non-attachment begins to emerge. A space opens up between you and the hand and even the process of looking at the hand. You realise that although you are looking at the hand, it's not particularly your hand and it's most definitely not you looking.

Eye gazing

Sit quietly and gaze into a mirror at your eyes. Again, just witness and maybe even label the process 'Looking', as before. The eyes stare straight back at you but after a while, again a distance begins to emerge between you, the observer and subject, the eyes. The eyes are part of your body; the act of looking is also part of your body — they are not you. You are the observer, you are separate and different from what is being perceived.

Body gazing

We can do the same when looking at the whole of the body. Try if you can to stand in front of a full height mirror and simply gaze towards the whole of your body. Not in a narcissistic or judgemental way, just as a non-attached observer. The same thing will happen after a few moments of intent gazing. A distance forms between you and the body. Don't try and search for this experience, it will come simply by the act of witnessing and you will certainly know when it happens in the body, as a feeling of effortlessness and lightness begins to emerge from the inside out.

Try these exercises often. You might recognise the experience that begins to unfold. You may already begin to feel and know this experience in your meditation.

This simple observation exercise leads us to knowing a fundamental fact regarding who we really are and what we are really made of. We discover that we are not our body, neither are we the senses, modes of perception, or judgement. Is the hand you've been gazing at really you? Are those eyes really you? Is your body really you? Are you this thing that's staring back at you from the mirror?

Well, no, you are something so much more.

To put all this into perspective and to give some guidance as to where we are going with our practice, we can extend this ability to observe everything we do. For example when walking, ask, 'is it me that is walking?' No is the answer. It is your body that is walking, you are simply the observer. You are watching the body walk. Similarly, when thinking, is it you that is thinking? Again, no is the answer. It is your mind that is thinking. You are sitting, watching the mind think.

Of course you can extend this to other observations directed towards the Doing field, such as I am not my status, my money, my possessions, my friends etc. But don't be alarmed — this doesn't mean that we're giving everything up and retreating from responsibilities, relationships, ambitions and intentions. It's just that when we learn to observe and disentangle any sense of identification and attachment with objects in the Doing field, we see them as they really are. You will notice that inhabiting this new - found inner space helps you to feel so much better.

And so our practice brings us full circle to where we started. To knowing life in the centre of our Being field. That felt sense of being is nourished and supported by knowing when we are in the centre. This takes us right back to the quote from Jack Hawley that I included at the beginning of this journey.

"Meditation... it's the bliss that comes with experiencing not mere happiness but complete satisfaction with the way things are..."

We aim to be connecting closely with our sense of Being, understanding the messages that come from the centre of consciousness. The more we read and understand those messages, the more we stay in our centre, in our sense of Being, in our essential nature. This helps us profoundly. We have ourselves an anchor that holds us in place, a point orientation, to help us navigate a viewpoint from which to see ourselves clearly as we venture outwards into the world through our Doing.

Introducing Being into your practice

We will often get a sense of Being many times during the day. With meditation practice, you will be able to switch on that sense of Being at will and apply it to where you are and what you're doing. But the sense of Being arises involuntarily too. Think about the times when you have been very busy carrying out a multitude of different tasks. That moment when you completed one task and before undertaking the next you took a little moment of stillness. A time out to collect your mind-body into the present. A moment of stillness in the middle of action. Do you remember how you felt, how the body rested, how the mind for a moment or two just reflected the world back to you, in the present, untroubled, calm, purposeful and ready?

Practice: Being Meditation

This meditation will take you into a deeper, more intimate space of self-enquiry. However, remember our intention is not direct self-analysis or examination. Instead, as you begin to develop and reside in your awareness space, we are going to take some time to explore a particular space right at the core of your experience. We are not looking for anything in particular; instead we are just developing insight as one begins to nurture a sense of Being at the centre. You may find this practice familiar. It's just that this time our intention is to identify and know our innate sense of Being.

In our previous Knowing meditation, our intention was to try and be open to an inner space of momentum. Now our intention is to go to that source of Knowing at the core of you.

- As before, settle into your formal meditation position and come into your alert and relaxed posture.

- Start by checking into the body, utilising your noticing technique, beginning with the fingers and toes. Observe the body for a moment without any judgement or preconception. Just be with the body and remind yourself that everything flows.

- From here you may wish to extend your meditation practice through all of the different objects or just utilise one or two that arise in the moment.

- Once you are resting in your space of awareness, allow yourself to explore these different dimensions of experience from each inquiry. Don't feel that you need to explore all of them in one practice. Let them come.

Where?

We start with Noticing. Where is your body located. What sort of space. Do you feel as if you are contained in that space or is there no sense of boundaries? Does your sense of Being feel non-specific, open, spacious everywhere but nowhere at the same time? Your sense of place is paradoxically established in one moment: **I am both inside and outside. In the physical body and yet also unbound by it.**

When?

As you settle into the practice, notice how as simply Being bends and distorts your experience of time. You may have intermittent experiences of simply resting and being in the now without any notions of past or future. And even the experience of now begins to fall as mental activity begins to settle.
I am outside of thought, time, space and my invented self.

How?

Now as you rest in your sense of Being, feel that you are complete just as you are. There seems to be nothing more that your mind-body needs. Wants and desires that may have been present at the start of your practice begin to lose their colour. They begin to fall away as your sense of Being is whole and complete experience grows. You seem to know that nothing more is needed in this moment.
I am fine beyond needs, wants or desires.

What?

You may discover that this feeling of Being is familiar. It's something you have always known, although perhaps never really acknowledged. If it is familiar, that's because it is. It's you, the real you. Your authentic self, full of potential, creativity and purpose and just waiting to be experienced, known and utilised.
I am complete: familiar, without need of reference.

We have arrived, although of course there is no real destination. But the more and more we rest in our innate sense of being we are nurturing and expanding this fundamental human capacity.

When you begin to connect the mind and body through meditation and align to where you are and what you are doing, you begin to discover your best self, that part of you which has been there all the time but has mostly remained hidden from view. Your best self, or in yogic terms your real Self, knows how to meet the moment creatively, in harmony with the world and expressed in everything you do.

Now it's time to use it and put it to work in the world.

9. Doing

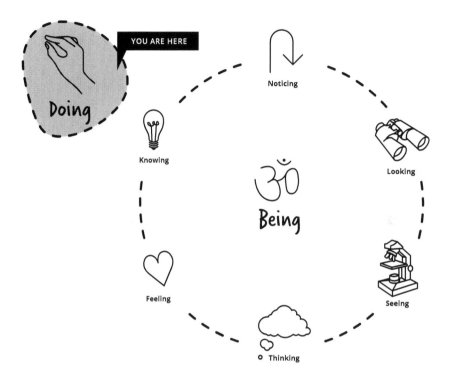

Fig 27. Doing. Where you can discover what you can really do.

In this final part, we find ourselves back out in the world outside our circle and in the world of action – the Doing field. Here we examine the output of meditation practice and how it's applied to modern everyday activity. If Being is our knowing of pure consciousness through meditation, then Doing is the manifestation of pure consciousness into the world. To do that, we need to know how to be open and make everything we do a meditation.

Here, we begin to bring everything into one experience through what we do. In our practice we have begun to nurture insight, direct our attention inwards and rest in a deeper sense of ourselves. Now with Doing, we are reaching back out into the world, again linking our Being with our Doing and becoming a vessel or a channel for a deeper, more authentic, profound version of ourselves.

Spontaneous action

As a young architect and after about two or three years of regular yoga practice, I began to notice a newly-emerging dimension to how I approached my work. I discovered what I called 'spontaneous response'. My work-related stress and anxiety began to fall away and in its place something started to unfold. An insight into where I was, what I was doing and more importantly **how** I was doing what I was doing.

I began to realise the state of oneness, wholeness and absorption, a total connection that I was beginning to uncover in my yoga and meditation practice, could in fact be taken off the mat and into the world outside. I began to feel the connection between being present, creativity, happiness and work and I could switch it on at will. I realised this was the whole point. To take what I was learning in my yoga and meditation class about myself and how I operated and functioned at a deeper level and then apply it out in the real world.

Pretty soon I began to notice that my most productive and insightful moments and when I was happiest were when I engaged more with the spontaneous and intuitive side of work. This meant drawing and designing without thinking or having expectations about the outputs.

I knew what needed to be done. I knew the timescales, the budgets, the constraints and limitations. But these would be located somewhere in the back of my mind, ready to be used when needed to check and fine-tune the process. Moments where I was paralysed or stuck, not knowing what to do, no longer seemed to be my problem. I could always come up with a solution. I began to realise that this way of working was intimately connected to what I was discovering through my yoga and meditation practice. I could **watch** myself work and thus free myself from self-generated, stressful, paralysing thoughts around fear of failure, lack of ability and expectation. It was my connection to the process, as it was happening in the moment and not some imagined, future product or outcome, that set me free.

I was being a conduit, getting out of the way, letting the workflow and process define and shape what had to be done in that moment. I could feel it in the mind-body field. Something was happening. Touch, movement, even the way I held myself in relation to what I was doing, all seemed effortless and easy.

Underneath was a feeling of joy. A joy defined simply as in that moment everything was exactly as it should be and I was doing exactly what I should be doing. There was a momentum, an inner force. It was liberating.

It was my hand and the pen that was drawing, not me. I was a participant but not the doer. I could watch. I gained greater clarity, creativity and energy — this was the beginning for me. I began to notice that I could go under thoughts and not be limited by any thinking or expectation.

Attention without tension

This was applied concentration but without effort. Attention without tension. Directed attention via a knowing open awareness and not from critical analysis. With practice, I could find that instead of my mind wandering or being distracted, I could focus all of my energies directly to the task. At that point the feeling of being centred, or better still returning to the centre, began to rise. With practice, I could switch on this new experience.

Thoughts of oneself, as myself, disappeared. Instead one's whole experience was illuminated by the whole subject. And I could feel it and utilise it whenever required.

This was the secret to knowing and experiencing work beyond the mind, beyond any interfering sense of I. It was all connected to the 'how' and not the 'what', 'when' or 'why' of Doing. To work in this way opened up a new reality of Seeing, Being and Doing. Everything could change. Ideas would flow.

I began to make that shift of perception. With practice, I began to perceive the distinction between the Doing an the Being field described in key yoga and meditation texts as the 'Field and the Knower of the Field'. What had previously been opaque in my reading now revealed itself to me. I had got it! There was action, there was experiencing the action, (the Doing) and then there was the experiencer, (the Being). The Knower – That was me. The real me. And it was all down to not what was being done, but to how it was being done. This was meditation in action — the observer, the method of observation and what was being observed merged together.

In other words, my eye of intuition had been opened up with

meditation, instructions from my teacher, self-practice and progressive study through the books I was now beginning to understand. The Doing field, I realised, was in constant flux and change. Its nature was finite, nothing lasts and that's where all action was taking place. The act of observing meant I activated the seer, or Knower of the Doing field. That shift placed me into the centre of the circle, the point of intersection between the vertical and horizontal, into the heart of the Being field. This was why so many people who use this experience often report that the work or action they are seemingly performing spontaneously felt like there was another agent involved. That the work seemed to come through them, from somewhere else. It often felt like they were the facilitator, more than the author or the originator of the work.

And it flowed.

This flow is also what we experience in modern meditation. It's the experience by which we know Being and Doing are merging for purpose, creativity and happiness.

Our algorithm of **ha = be + do − I** is fully active. We are making happy work.

Getting into the flow of things

In this final part, our objective is to link the inner and outer circles of our map together. It's here that our inner and outer worlds merge where our Being and Doing fields overlap into one unified field experience.

To be whole and centred is the point of meditation. The idea is to bring into practice the insight and perspective that emerges.

When we are undertaking our sitting meditation practice, we are acting as an open receiver. We allow and welcome experiences to arise, persist for a moment and then fall. We don't act, fuse with or respond to each object experience, we simply observe without judgement. This rising and passing of objects into awareness is flow.

We expand from our experience of things happening to us, as they rise, stay and then fall away in our awareness, to being aware of experiences that now come from us being active and doing things. We are still maintaining and practicing our **sustained present moment awareness** but now in action rather than sitting and being still.

We focus on the action as it is, not on the imagined results. So in the same way we simply 'witnessed' breathing, sensation, hearing, thinking — we now apply that shift of perspective or attention to the action.

We are going to observe and label action now as a meditation object. Even though we are the **doer** (in terms of our mind-body field) of each action, we 'observe' it as an object, rising momentarily and then falling away.

We can use standing/walking/action/experience as our meditation object. We are witnessing the action-moment arising in the mind-body field. We are the observer, without judgement or expectation, this is just standing/walking etc.

Again, we employ the meditation technique. So walking is an action we can employ to extend the depth and impact of the practice. When you get it, meditative walking is wonderful. You will find walking flows, it becomes effortless, a whole mind-body experience, tinged with joy, momentum and purpose.

Doing Meditations

Core aspects of 'Doing' meditations are:

- Observing or witnessing oneself in action. Not just sitting and receiving but standing, acting and doing. The primary meditation object is simply the experience of action moment-to-moment.

- The aim is to let go of the feeling of 'I' as much as possible and merely know the bare, phenomenal experience of each moment/action/event as it is.

- Relaxing into a 'knowing' of experience rather than an interpretation or analytical description of what is happening. Let go, allow yourself to flow.

- An experience which combines both mental and physical, which then leads to an emerging experience of the mind–body field as a distinct experience separate from self.

- Leading to a sense of internal spaciousness and effortlessness.

Standing meditation

Like all the meditations, you can do this anywhere. You can either choose to do it formally at home, in work or informally as you go about your daily tasks. This, 'conscious standing', like the sitting meditation, will be a challenge, but with regular practice can be done almost anywhere — queuing in line at the bank, at the pedestrian crossing, on your commute, in lifts — or if you want, simply standing in your meditation space.

We often call this meditation the **Post Office meditation** because it's ideal to do when you find yourself standing in line. Instead of standing in the queue with your mind and attention fixed solely on the head of the queue, allowing thoughts to be distracted with impatience, expectation, judgement and anger, with this meditation we are solely interested in the process of simply standing in the moment.

Just like the sitting meditation, engaging and connecting the mind-body field is important. Standing meditation requires you to stand with awareness and alertness allied with a relaxed attention. **The action and experience of standing becomes a meditation object.**

Standing meditation develops a greater awareness of the body — a clear sense of orientation in space. The act of standing mindfully draws your attention towards the sensations in the body and immediacy of Being and Doing moment-by-moment.

Practice: Standing meditation

Preparation

- Place feet flat on the floor, hip-width apart, toes pointing forward. The intention is to feel grounded and rooted to the floor.

- Draw in the knees to your centre line gently so the legs activate and flex. The legs and feet push downwards into the floor supporting the feeling of being 'connected' to the ground.

- Drop the arms down alongside the body. Ensure the hands are relaxed but the fingertips are very gently flexed pointing down towards the floor.

- Relax the shoulders. Open the chest and gently lift the crown of the head upwards (a gentle elevation of the spine).

- Only close your eyes if it's safe to do so. If you are doing this in a public space, keep the eyes open but softly gazing forward.

- Notice now a balance between the upward lift of the upper body (into space) and the downward push of the lower body (into the ground).

The Meditation

- Begin by settling into the body. You can switch on your Noticing technique with the fingers and toes and gradually expand your body awareness to include your whole body.

- As you begin to occupy the body in this posture, open up your attention towards the breath and just watch the body breathing for you for a moment.

- Bring your attention to the body standing. Acknowledge that it is not you that is standing, it is the body standing for you. There is no one standing. I am not standing, we are not standing, there is simply standing.

- Just watch. Label this 'standing'. The body is standing for you, you don't need to make it happen.

- Feel your feet rooting into the ground. Feel the legs push downwards, connecting you to the ground. Now bring your attention upwards through the body. Maybe you can feel the chest, the back lift upwards. Maybe you can feel the chest open. Feel the shoulders relax and the head lift.

- Notice how the body is standing for you. Notice how the mind-body is working to keep you upright. Feel the sway, relax, be still, balanced and steady.

- Stay with it. Don't change or shape anything. Just let go...

- Continue to label the experience without expectation or judgement. Mentally repeat 'standing, standing, I'm not standing...'

- If there are new feelings coming through, in the legs or the back, just be with them, repeat the standing label.

- To end your standing meditation, gently move the body but stay with the emerging experience for as long as you can. Stretch if you need to. Then continue with your day.

Walking meditation

I try and practice walking meditation as often as possible. At least twice a day walking the dog and as often as I can walking to class, or even moving around the house.

After standing meditation, walking meditation begins to reveal a changing of the mind's relationship to what is happening and it begins to open you up to an effortless flow. Now, instead of the body being still and being an open receiver to experience, the mind-body is now also the originator of the action creating the experience. The body is aware of moving. You are aware of that awareness.

If you've ever researched mindful or meditative walking, you're sure to have found a myriad of complex techniques and practices. Rather than deliver a mindful walk, these techniques mostly serve to overcomplicate what is a wonderful opportunity to merge Being and Doing. As soon as you call a walk 'mindful', you run the risk of feeling self-conscious, somehow exaggerating your movement. That's not mindful walking, that's self-conscious walking.

Effective walking meditation is first and foremost not defined as such. That's the whole point. As soon as you say 'I am now doing a mindful walk', it's not mindful. Meditation is a cognitive shift of perception. It's a state where we are being aware of being aware, or better still noticing and paying attention, without wondering what your mind and body are doing, moment-to-moment. Remove labels, definitions and imagined outcomes and just go with the process, or as we sometimes say, go with the flow. So when is walking just walking? Not 'I am walking', or 'I am mindfully walking'. You are witnessing the action-moment arising in the mind-body field. You are the observer, without judgement or expectation... just walking.

Other applications

After a while, with practice you can experiment applying the **beanddo** algorithm to a whole range of different things, experiences, events, actions and so on. Genuinely anything can be a meditation experience and used as an object — filling in spreadsheets, attending meetings, giving presentations, shopping, the view from your window, reading, swimming, running, even just sitting down and breathing, as we have seen. All of these objects are in themselves not meditations. They are simply vehicles to allow us to occupy our Being field as it merges with our Doing field.

Being and Doing are no longer separate, they are one where all self awareness is reduced. We become free from our own mental conditioning. Fear, expectation, worry, anxiety, jealousy, all aspects of ourselves which are normally unconscious, all fade away for that moment leaving just a joyous, gratifying, pure insightful awareness.

10. Final thoughts

Take inspired action

We often conclude our meditation classes with an invitation for everyone to get out there and **'save the world'**. This would seem an ambitious instruction but our mission at **beanddo** is to do just that — to change the world with, and through you. It would be pointless not to have such a bold ambition when it comes to this ancient life-affirming practice.

When you make a decision to change, the world changes with you.

"We're not on a journey to save the world but to save ourselves. However, in doing that you save the world. The influence of a vital person vitalizes."[16]

Modern meditation is no less than the transformation of consciousness. Or better still, a realisation of consciousness in the world. When we practice, we work on ourselves in order to have a deeper and thorough conscious experience. We know that this transformation helps people experience meaning, purpose and creativity in their lives as they become compassionate, positive agents of change in their workplace, their homes and their communities.

---

16   *The Power of Myth, Joseph Campbell with Bill Moyers*

There is an old yoga maxim, **'Be in the world, not of it!'** This is another way of describing that inner shift of perspective and perception we've talked about in this book. In a world of action, of constant momentum, this is the secret to living a creative life of real achievements and purpose. This is the role of modern meditation, to help you be in the world but liberated and free — free to be exactly who you are, doing what you need to do. To be 'field – independent' as we often say in our **beanddo** classes.

The whole purpose has been to rest in the heart of who we are. To connect to one's essential nature, to the source of who you are, before it's too late and let it flow. After all, that's what it's designed to do. It's often the case that our own assumptions and misconceptions get in the way and limit or even stop this flow. Ultimately, we are responsible for seeing the world clearly and seeing the endless possibilities it offers for a creative, fulfilling and thriving life.

We often say in class, **"If the world begins to change for you, it's not because it has, it's because *you* are changing."** With practice, you open up to a new perception of the world, who you are and what you can do. We said at the beginning of this book that meditation is simply a shift of perspective.

It's a purposeful shift which brings you to being fully aware and awake. In yoga practice, we might call this **enlightenment.** It comes in many shapes and sizes. It brings you to your senses — literally. You know at last that you're alive, in this moment, having this experience, in this body, knowing that everything you need you already have.

From here then, the only choice is to take inspired action.

Modern meditation will set you free. With practice, you will find that when you link to that inner stillness - that sense of Being - you will discover all the tools and resources needed to help you deal with negative patterns of thinking. Whether that's the limiting inner critic, and sense of self doubt, or a persistent nagging feeling of anxiety in the pit of your stomach, or that rush of stress and apprehension every time your mobile rings or an email drops into your inbox. Many challenges - however big or small - can be tackled with the intuition modern meditation gives us.

At the beginning of this book I talked about reconnecting with that inner space, that part of you which is safe, comforting, reassuring and nourishing, which I call coming home. To feel at home is, in the end, what we are all longing for.

This search for home was what has shaped much of my career as an architect. I worked to create space, manipulate light and shape form in a meaningful way. That is the stuff of architecture — memory, function, history, context, value, all merged together to create what we architects like to call a sense of place in an effort to try and reconnect, to make an experience of connection. I realise now that it can only ever be partially successful, as one can only go so far in shaping the external world. We have to shape our internal world too - as a matter of some urgency.

This book is not the solution. It can only serve as a map, a set of instructions, waymarkers, touchpoints along your inner journey. If there is one thing I have realised over the last 25 years, it is that it's all about practice, practice, practice and more practice. So, in the end, everything you do can become a meditation. Everything you do becomes happy work. Hopefully you have realised now that you are happy. In reality, there is not a great deal externally that can bring you happiness. You have it already. The key is to make that your starting point. Because that's where all meditation begins. Change only happens in the now. With regular practice, you will notice what you are doing and what is getting in the way of knowing and optimising that. You realise it's not **what** we go through in life, it's **how** we go through life that makes all the difference.

The origins of **beanddo** are many. But one quote from David Lynch encapsulates our energy and direction:

"Stay true to yourself. Let your voice ring out, and don't let anybody fiddle with it. Never turn down a good idea, but never take a bad idea. And meditate. It's very important to experience that Self, that pure consciousness. It's really helped me... Grow in happiness and intuition. Experience the joy of doing. And you'll glow in this peaceful way. Your friends will be very, very happy with you. Everyone will want to sit next to you. And people will give you money!"[17]

It is then that we start to hear that inner voice. Not the voice in our head, which we work to help settle, but that deeper, softer voice of insight and guidance made of a language only you can understand. We must trust that inner teacher, that inner

---

17   *David Lynch. Catching the Big Fish: Meditation, Consciousness and Creativity*

architect that is normally covered over by all the noise and distractions. When we tune in and listen we make a direct connection to our inner consciousness, our essential nature, the source of who we are. To feel that creative force that flows through us and around us before a thought forms, an action takes place, a feeling emerges, a word is shaped.

It might seem by now that learning to meditate is a process of unlearning. We don't need to carry on being the person we thought we were, or were told we had to be, instead we just be. Then you will see the world as it really is. In spite of everything people do every day, we see that the world is essentially a playful, creative, evocative and inspiring place to be and not a problem that needs to be solved, shaped or manipulated. You and the world are already fit for purpose — **so start making happy work!**

MODERN MEDITATION
–
FREQUENTLY ASKED QUESTIONS

In this final part, I have set out some of the frequently asked questions many of our students raise. You might want to return to this final section regularly as your own practice grows and develops.

Getting started.

What do I need to start meditation practice?
The good news is, very little.

As long as you have a mind, body, breath and senses, a comfortable chair to sit in and a reasonably quiet place to practice, you are ready to go. The beauty of meditation is you already have everything you need.

At some point you will need to go to a good teacher. It's been done like that for thousands of years. Meditation, like deep relaxation, is something that you do; it's not something that is done to you.

When should I start?
Right here, right now.

No really; learning to meditate is a lot like learning to swim. You can learn the theory of swimming but until you get into the water you will never know what it's really like. It's exactly the same with meditation. The knowing of it and the learning of it is in the doing of it – so don't hesitate, don't think too much about it, jump in and start swimming. And just like swimming you feel your way into it; you can't rush it. And like swimming it's a whole body and mind experience. You just know when you get it. Get a good teacher, keep practicing and it will happen.

How should I start?
By remembering what brought you to this point.

What did you want to change – and why? Once you answer this, make it your intention to commit to your practice. Don't try too hard. Your experience is your experience. There is no right or wrong way – just your way.

How long should I meditate for?
Before you start, decide how long you want to practice for. If you are a beginner, you may want to try meditating for five or 10 minutes at a time. There are no targets to hit but try to aim for 20 minutes twice a day before breakfast and your evening meal. This may sound challenging but you will be surprised to find that you do have time if you plan for it.

You can extend the time you sit incrementally, but don't rush. You will find that once you get into your practice, time length will not be a concern as time perception drops away.

Don't worry if you miss a session. Accepting things as they are when they happen is key to meditation; simply look forward to your next session. To stop you from worrying about how long you've been meditating, set a timer. Most smartphones have one, or you can download a meditation timer app. Successfully practicing for a committed length of time will greatly increase your confidence.

This is not true for everyone but you may find that morning meditation is easier to do as the mind is calmer. In the evening, the mind and body can be agitated, irritated or more tired, making your practice more challenging – which is why you need to practice regularly.

Do I need to meditate in a special place?
Not particularly.

However, try and meditate regularly in a space that has good natural light and airflow. If you can, try and sit by a window although this is not vital. The important thing is to be in a space where you won't be disturbed. It doesn't need to be soundproof as occasional background sounds such as a passing aeroplane, traffic or wind are fine and sometimes beneficial. Sound can be used as a meditation object, as long as it's not too intrusive.

If you can, try and make a space for regular practice. Keep a special chair, have a nearby shelf with a selection of meaningful objects on it such as photographs, books or souvenirs from your favourite places. Creating a little space like this for your meditation will help you settle and focus inwards, strengthen your intention and lend a deeper significance to your practice.

What sort of posture should I adopt?
First and foremost, a comfortable one. As meditation starts with the body a good comfortable, purposeful posture will set conditions for meditation. If you have practiced yoga postures for years then you will have no trouble sitting cross-legged on a zafu (a meditation cushion) on the floor with your back reasonably straight and unsupported. This is not a prerequisite for meditation practice as a chair is just as effective. In meditation you will need to 'hold' your mind-body in a state of relaxed, effortless, ready alertness and awareness. This might sound like a contradiction but it can developed by being conscious of your posture, particularly at the start.

Do not practice meditation lying down, as it is very easy to fall asleep and inhibits the ability to build mind/body awareness. Do not meditate on a full stomach.

What do I wear?
You don't need anything special.

Comfortable, everyday clothes are fine. If you are in the office, you might want to loosen your collar and remove your jacket, remembering to always take off your shoes. If you wear glasses you might want to remove them. Some people also like to remove watches and jewellery, so do whatever feels right for you. If you practice on a hard chair, it's often a good idea to have a cushion available to sit on or place in your lower back. Being comfortable so that you can build your awareness is the main requirement.

What should I do at the end of my practice?
Take your time.

Gently open your eyes. Try not to focus on anything in particular, just allow the light in as you raise your eyelids. Sit quietly for a few moments; don't rush to get up straight away. This is a moment to enjoy how the world comes back to you bit by bit and perhaps with a little more clarity. If something particular came up in your meditation practice, just acknowledge it for a few moments, rather than dwell on it. If it's important, write it down. It's often a good idea to keep a notebook and pen handy. Just notice how you feel, make a mental note and try to maintain it for as long as you can before you become distracted by the next event of the day.

What will it feel like?
This is a difficult question to answer, as the experience will be different for everyone.

Meditation is easy and natural and scientists are now

realising that our brains seem to be hardwired towards developing the benefits of meditation. You may have noticed in the past when, in your still quiet moments, you felt an open-flowing awareness, sudden flashes of insight or feelings of being, present, whole and centred. They just arise as if from nowhere, combined with moments of happiness and joy not connected to anything external. You may then have let those experiences pass or fall away without paying much attention, as you became distracted by something happening externally. Meditation is a technique for sustaining that deeper experience by focusing and holding your attention inwards, towards that pure-flowing awareness.

It's a subtle, intuitive experience but after a while that flowing, joyful feeling will stay with you and you can learn to switch it on whenever you want. Humans have been practicing it for well over 5000 years. It's tried and tested and it works!

What is meant by noticing and checking in?
Being here now!

Stopping and checking in is a way to help focus and prepare the ground for meditation practice. Treat it like a personal 'threshold', a point at which the day's events, planned or past, are put to one side in favour of being here now and ready for meditation.

Be aware of your mood as you begin to practice. As your increase awareness emerges, use it to help you direct your attention inwards towards your stillness, no matter how hard it feels. Don't feel despondent on the days it feels as though little progress has been made or you feel you just don't get it. Persevere: it works.

What is a meditation object?

Meditation objects are event and experiential phenomena that rise and fall or pass through your awareness. When we change our relationship to them through meditation practice, our expansive awareness unfolds. Objects are essentially everything that is not your awareness.

All objects are said to be 'known' while your awareness is the 'knower'. Meditation science says that we are ultimately not our mind, body, action or experience. They belong to us but they are not us. When we know this we can learn to watch and witness everything that happens in our mind and the world around us as objects, allowing us to change our relationship to what we see, feel and do by cultivating non-attachment or non-judgement.

Objects are the body, breath, sensation, hearing, thinking and any action. With practice you will begin to feel relaxed, still and very present by being able to 'switch on' this body awareness at any time.

What is meant by 'following my breath'?

Like the body, the breath is a useful meditation object because it's always present. To follow the breath means to be aware of it, watch and monitor it but not seek to alter or change it in any way. You need to let go and relax, allowing the breath to be just as it is. This will take practice because as we direct our attention to the breath, the mind will seek to interfere. This is why we must learn to watch the breath.

Following the breath and then labelling the experience of each breath as it rises and falls is central to open monitoring meditation (OM meditation). It is a primary practice and one you will turn to regularly.

When can I expect results?
The point of meditation is not to expect anything! To make progress you need to practice regularly but don't expect or desire results. Try to cultivate 'effortless effort', get out of the way and 'be' the practice rather than 'apply' it.

This way you find that the deeper teachings will unfold. Learn the techniques and practice but also be open to the subtleties and tone of new experience. Practice with an open heart and be receptive to everything. Know that meditation practice taps into your inner knowing (your intuition). Let the different aspects of knowledge, practice and technique sink in and it will become clear. Meditation practice will help you open up and move beyond your intellectual understanding of experience. It will link you to a deeper, intuitive and more conscious awareness.

Will meditation change me?
Yes. With practice you will notice:

· That being present in the here and now reveals how the world really is and what you need to do in it.

· An emerging and empowering sense, in tune with your inner nature and being.

· How to properly relax, let go and reduce stress, anxiety and fear and to simply be still.

· How to trust intuition and direct your natural, spontaneous creativity and flow.

· That you can be an effective and inspiring leader and help empower others.

- You will deepen your day-to-day experience and manifest your personal goals.

- How to live skillfully and learn how to respond fruitfully to your thoughts, events and other people.

- The ability to switch on your self-awareness, focus and concentration.

- Know how to incorporate meditation into everyday life and know the joy of doing.

What are the key principles?

Meditation is a simple process of directing and maintaining your attention to the present. You learn to watch your thoughts, feelings and experiences objectively, in an open non-judgemental way without analysis or attachment. This leads to a heightened experience that helps you to live in the moment. This way, life doesn't pass you by unrecognised; you see things as they really are, not what you think they are. These experiences enable you to live and work effortlessly, creatively and joyfully.

- The word meditation simply means 'to attend'. All you do is turn up, pay attention to where you are and what you are doing without wanting to change things. This takes regular practice.

- Meditation is not about forcing anything to happen. All the good stuff happens when you master the art of not trying.

- It's not about stopping or suppressing your thoughts; it's about having a different relationship to them.

- You don't need to recite a mantra, sit in an awkward posture or follow any doctrine.

- It takes practice and commitment; meditation isn't a quick fix but it is a lasting one.

- Anyone can meditate, anywhere at any time. That's the whole point. It's starts in the real world with you.

- Meditation practice will reduce stress, anxiety and fear. It works directly on the brain and nervous system. You don't need to adopt a different lifestyle. But you will notice benefits and positive changes in your everyday activities.

Overcoming Challenges

What if I can't feel my body?
Don't worry, you will.

Many people are not particularly body aware because most the time they are locked solely into their heads. Meditation practice helps to unlock that habit so that reconnection with the whole body is possible, promoting an experience of being, moment by moment.

To build your body awareness, you will need to practice noticing or body scanning. This is a yoga technique (used for relaxation and yoga nidra). As you sit bring your attention to your fingers and then your toes. Don't look at them or move them. Just bring your attention there. After a short while you will become aware of a subtle and gentle sensation in the fingers and toes as your nervous system is stimulated and energy starts to flow. Your extremities are very sensitive to your attention. Focus on the sensation without judging or forcing it. Just let it be as it is. Then after a while work towards growing and extending the sensation upwards through the arms and legs until you can sense the whole body as it is in the chair. Don't worry if there are areas that do not respond. That is common; just go where your body and mind allow you to go. Allowing the sensation to flow is how you direct and expand your attention and developing your own body consciousness.

What do I do with particular thoughts?
Nothing.

Following or examining a particular train of thought in meditation is not useful and will only distract you. The objective of your practice is to create a 'space' between you and your thoughts and any particular reaction prompted by the thought. Certain patterns of negative thinking and how it impacts how you feel will be apparent as you practice. You do not need to cross-examine your thinking in an effort to limit it. You will notice as you practice that you are preparing the ground and planting the seeds for good positivity to naturally grow. Keep faith with the practice of simply 'watching' your thoughts as objects as they come and go. Once you manage to simply observe your thoughts without judgement or analysis they will settle. Your thoughts do not go away but, as your relationship with them changes, you will notice that they will fall into the background, while in the foreground a deeper sense of stillness emerges.

My mind is always busy. What if I can't control it?
That is the point of meditation.

Your mind is busy. It's thinking most of the time, but if we try to control it, it will only get worse. Meditation is not mind control. We are not trying to switch the mind off, but switch it on!

Meditation is a change of perspective. A shift in how you observe and react to your mental activity. When we learn through practice, to sit alongside or underneath our flow of thoughts and simply 'witness' them as they come and go, you will notice the mind will settle naturally without effort or force. It takes practice but you will feel this shift happen all by itself. Trying to stop thinking is impossible, it's like trying to stop breathing; it can't be done. So instead what we do is accept what is going on in our head and then use meditation techniques to change our relationship to our thinking. Remember: you are not your thoughts. Once we realise the implications of this we can change and shift our perspective.

What if my mind is always wandering?
That's fine, that's what it does.

The point of meditation is that we notice when the mind has wandered away from where we want it to be. Many people don't notice where the mind is going or has gone to. They just follow, allowing their mind to create assumptions, beliefs and frameworks, as it constantly gets caught up with distractions. A great moment in one's meditation journey is to realise that the mind has become distracted. With practice, you bring it back to the present moment.

What if I can't sit still for so long?
You can; you will surprise yourself. It's important not to force yourself to be still. That's why you should start with sitting for short periods. As you learn to relax, focus inwards and develop a body awareness you will notice that the body will remain still for longer periods.

Fidgeting is a sign of excess energy and an agitated mind. Meditation practice will eventually balance energy flow and settle the mind, naturally stopping fidgeting.

What if I fall asleep?
Don't worry that happens sometimes.

Many people will fall asleep in meditation, particularly in the evening. Your sitting posture will help you to stay awake. A useful technique is to meditate with the upper eyelids gently lifted, allowing a little light in. You won't be able to see anything clearly, other than your body as you sit in the chair. This technique also helps you focus forwards into the space between your eyebrows. If feeling sleepy becomes a problem, just gently bring your practice to an end, wait a few moments, get up and carry on with your day.

What if I get emotional?
That can happen.

Some people report feelings of either positive or negative emotion arising during or after meditation practice. Don't worry, this is perfectly normal. As you begin to relax, let go and open your experience, many of the unconscious restrictions and resistance you have unwittingly nurtured over the years to deal with certain feelings begin to loosen. No matter what comes up, understand that it is a sign of positive change and growth.

Sometimes, you will find yourself getting tearful for seemingly no apparent reason. Again, this is a good thing. The process of meditation is often referred to as removers of obstacles, so any emotions and feelings that are experienced are simply the clearing away of deeply-rooted issues. Some people also report the resurfacing of certain childhood memories. Again, this is normal as the body/mind remembers when you last experienced profound moments of happiness and joy, often when we were young.

FREQUENTLY ASKED QUESTIONS

How do I deal with pain and discomfort?
By simply watching and not reacting.

The point is to be comfortable. Do not sit on the floor crossed-legged unless you are used to it. Using a chair will minimise discomfort. Remember to use all experience as a chance to meditate. If any pain or discomfort arises (and it will) convert it into a meditation object. Simply watch and witness the feeling without judgement or one's relationship to it. For example, instead of thinking 'I am feeling pain', simply replace the knowing of it as 'sensation'. After a while, the experience will fall away into the background. Of course if it's too painful, change your posture.

A last piece of advice...

Get in the water and start swimming. Embrace your meditation teaching and delight in your practice. With this mindset, you will notice from day one how things can be different.

ACKNOWLEDGEMENTS

Acknowledgements go firstly to my wife and best friend Sue, who has made **beanddo** possible while also being the sharpest critic and wonderful lifetime collaborator in just about everything I see, think, feel, know and do.

I am also blessed to be sharing this journey with most inspiring friends and teachers, particularly Anna K, my 'ancient yogi' whose love, insight and thoughtfulness drives our ambition. I am also so indebted to Katy R, who edited this book. Her professionalism, knowledge and patience with an architect who draws better than he writes has been vital to making this idea real.

I am also hugely grateful to family and friends who more or less volunteered to test and check the content of this work, particularly Briony G, Mike P, Ian D, Mark E and Jax S who in their own unique way are making happy work.

Thank you to all of my students who turned out to be the best possible teachers, including everyone on our teaching training programmes and the **beanddo** Learning Circle. This stuff doesn't happen without you!

And finally a huge thank you goes to Sophie, Hannah and Tom at Placemarque who designed the look and feel of **beanddo** and to Sophie who designed this book.

FURTHER READING
AND EXPLORATION

You can download some of the techniques and practices I describe in this book as guided meditations. Go to:

http://www.beanddo.co.uk/guided-meditations.html

There is an old yoga adage regarding reading about yoga. Firstly, don't take anybody's word for it, find out for yourself. Experience it directly. Secondly, it's often said that when it comes to yoga and meditation, an ounce of practice is worth a tonne of theory. Having said that, I have listed a few books here that might just help you.

We use some of these books in our unique **beanddo** teacher training programme.

Core texts

At some stage you may wish to explore where meditation comes from. I have listed below the two core texts. These versions are very user-friendly and are recommended on our teacher training course. As with all things like this, don't worry about trying to get the core teaching straight away. You won't! But strangely, the more you continue to develop your practice, the more the insights in the teaching become increasingly less opaque and obscure. After a while you will get it!

Effortless Being: The Yoga Sutras of Patanjali. Alistair Shearer (1982)

The Bhagavad Gita: A Walkthrough for Westerners. Jack Hawley (2001)

Teach Us To Sit Still: A Sceptic's Search for Health and Healing. Tim Parks (2010)

Tim Parks is an absolute beginner to meditation. In fact, it's so alien to his normal day-to-day world as a well-known writer, his experiences here are all the more revealing to anyone who is thinking of diving into meditation. He learns a guided relaxation technique, which for him is a revelation. Parks describes what happens next with great humour and honesty. If you are new to meditation, this is a sceptic's analysis that turns out to be one of the best messages on why we all need to bring meditation into our lives before it's too late.

Catching the Big Fish: Meditation, Consciousness and Creativity. David Lynch (2006)

A hero at **beanddo**, David Lynch's Catching the Big Fish is funny, insightful and illuminating. You have to know Lynch's character a little and be familiar with his delivery. It's style is clipped and direct. But it is an easy read. He's also not afraid to come at you with some big concepts on consciousness, creativity and where ideas come from (they are the Big Fish). There is not a great deal here on technique; he leaves that to others. Lynch is more concerned about why we need to meditate and what happens in your day-to-day world when you do. Lynch says that meditation reveals the joy of doing; the impact of your practice on others and how the world becomes a brighter better place.

Inner Engineering: A Yogi's Guide to Joy. Sadhguru (2016)

Sadhguru is often described as a modern day guru. Don't be put off by appearances — the long white beard and hair, the scarves and robes. This is a motor biking, Everton-supporting, coffee-drinking yogi who really gets it. Yoga and meditation for him is a science that we adapt and apply. Sadhguru talks about his own journey in terms of how he learned not to be 'enslaved' by external events. He tells us that the 'here and now' is the only thing that matters because that is where everything is. If we spend all our time being distracted, we miss out on life. And we couldn't agree more.

Mindfulness In Plain English. Bhante Henepola Gunaratana (2002)
Gunaratana describes with brilliant clarity how to get down and practice meditation. Here is a yogi meditator at the peak of his teaching powers with a clear description of what is involved. This is the real thing!

The Power of Now: A Guide to Spiritual Enlightenment. Eckhart Tolle (2001)
This bestseller will take you further into your meditation practice. But to really get it, you need to practice too. Meditation practice, Tolle says, bring that realisation that you and the now are the same thing and that they exist together in a profound and unmanifested spatial stillness and peace, creativity and flow. The Power of Now is really all about you right here, right now. Knowing that changes everything. This is a beautifully-written, poetic book.

35196968R00110

Printed in Poland
by Amazon Fulfillment
Poland Sp. z o.o., Wrocław